Lean Retailing

By Ade Asefeso MCIPS MBA

Copyright 2014 by Ade Asefeso MCIPS MBA
All rights reserved.

First Edition

ISBN-13: 978-1502762290

ISBN-10: 1502762293

Publisher: AA Global Sourcing Ltd
Website: http://www.aaglobalsourcing.com

Table of Contents

Disclaimer 5
Dedication 6
Chapter 1: Introduction 7
Chapter 2: Lean Manufacturing Needs Lean Retailers 11
Chapter 3: Challenges and Opportunities in Retail Sector 15
Chapter 4: Lean Warehousing and Distribution Centre 21
Chapter 5: Lean Retailing and Inventory Control 33
Chapter 6: Lean Supply Chain 37
Chapter 7: Lean IT in Retail Sector 43
Chapter 8: The Effects of Lean in Retail 47
Chapter 9: Lean Consumption 55
Chapter 10: Lean in Retail Sector 59
Chapter 11: Applying Lean Thinking in the Retail Sector 61
Chapter 12: Effective Retail Manager 73
Chapter 13: Using Lean in Retail Stores 77
Chapter 14: Using Lean to Reduce Employee Turnover 81
Chapter 15: Reducing Cost and Optimizing Service 87
Chapter 16: Lean Retail is About Time and Money 95
Chapter 17: Tips for Optimising Your Return 99

Chapter 18: Making Fashion Retailers More Sustainable..101
Chapter 19: Retail Values for Lean Leadership...107
Chapter 20: Building a Lean Culture in Retail Distribution Operation 109
Chapter 21: From Lean to Lasting........................115
Chapter 22: Conclusion 127

Disclaimer

This publication is designed to provide competent and reliable information regarding the subject matter covered. However, it is sold with the understanding that the author and publisher are not engaged in rendering professional advice. The authors and publishers specifically disclaim any liability that is incurred from the use or application of contents of this book.

If you purchased this book without a cover you should be aware that this book may have been stolen property and reported as "unsold and destroyed" to the publisher. In this case neither the author nor the publisher has received any payment for this "stripped book."

Dedication

To my family and friends who seems to have been sent here to teach me something about who I am supposed to be. They have nurtured me, challenged me, and even opposed me…. But at every juncture has taught me!

This book is dedicated to my lovely boys, Thomas, Michael and Karl. Teaching them to manage their finance will give them the lives they deserve. They have taught me more about life, presence, and energy management than anything I have done in my life.

Chapter 1: Introduction

Lean core idea is to maximize customer value while minimizing waste. Simply, Lean means creating more value for customers with fewer resources.

A Lean organization understands customer value and focuses its key processes to continuously increase it. The ultimate goal is to provide perfect value to the customer through a perfect value creation process that has zero waste.

To accomplish this, Lean thinking changes the focus of management from optimizing separate technologies, assets, and vertical departments to optimizing the flow of products and services through entire value streams that flow horizontally across technologies, assets, and departments to customers.

Eliminating waste along entire value streams, instead of at isolated points, creates processes that need less human effort, less space, less capital, and less time to make products and services at far less costs and with much fewer defects, compared with traditional business systems. Companies are able to respond to changing customer desires with high variety, high quality, low cost, and with very fast throughput times. Also, information management becomes much simpler and more accurate.

A popular misconception is that Lean is suited only for manufacturing. Not true. Lean applies in every business and every process. It is not a tactic or a cost reduction program, but a way of thinking and acting for an entire organization.

Businesses in all industries and services, including Retailing, Healthcare and Governments, are using Lean principles as the way they think and do. Many organizations choose not to use the word Lean, but to label what they do as their own system, such as the Toyota Production System. Why? To drive home the point that Lean is not a program or short term cost reduction program, but the way the company operates. The word transformation or Lean transformation is often used to characterize a company moving from an old way of thinking to Lean thinking. It requires a complete transformation on how a company conducts business. This takes a long-term perspective and perseverance.

Lean retailing is an emerging trend that will soon force manufacturers to build standard products on-demand using spontaneous build-to-order techniques. Power has shifted from manufacturers to Lean retailers, such as Wal-Mart, Lands' End, Dillard's, Federated Department Stores (Macy's, Bloomingdale's), The Gap, J. C. Penny, Sears Roebuck and Tesco. These powerful retailers now insist on rock-bottom prices and refuse to carry inventory, expecting manufacturers to provide rapid and frequent replenishment of retail products based on real-time sales.

Manufacturers who resist change will make their first attempts to satisfy Lean retailers from inventory made in forecasted production but, this is will always be sub-optimal because inventory and its management adds cost and poses an endless dilemma, which will get worse as forecasts become less accurate.

Savvy manufacturers will dominate this market with Spontaneous Build-to-Order which can deliver products on-demand without forecasts or inventory. This reduces or eliminates all the costs associated with inventory, obsolescence, and distribution in addition to easily providing rapid and frequent deliveries to distribution centres or even directly to stores.

Chapter 2: Lean Manufacturing Needs Lean Retailers

If the Leanest possible manufacturer of consumer products approached some big retailers with the proposition that they could provide very low cost products, with excellent quality, in small quantities to each store, with very short lead times, and could even customize the products to a certain extent such that the customers in each region could get exactly what they want, that manufacturer would be sent away empty handed because the buyers of big retailers are not interested.

Stuck in their outdated business model, with a simple minded economic model, they all scour the globe looking for a supplier they can wring a few cents out of on the purchase price, then send the product in staggering quantities through the most bloated and wasteful supply chains.

The silliness of big retail in an increasingly Lean manufacturing world can be most easily understood if one can imagine a Toyota dealer ignoring Toyota manufacturing capability. Picture a Toyota dealer only offering custom ordered cars with six week lead times, ignoring the fact that Toyota can actually get the car to him within a week or two. Imagine him trying to squeeze every customer for a few more bucks for an 'extended warranty' instead of using the fact that one isn't needed as the product's strongest feature. Imagine him renting extra space to keep a couple hundred extra cars in his inventory, just in case, and passing the cost of the inventory on to his customers; because in that supply chain the manufacturer rules, a Toyota dealer who did business in such an insane manner would either shape up or lose the franchise. In most retail supply chains, however, the retail buyer is king. Unfortunately, there are few places in the business world in which so much authority is placed in such incompetent hands. (Wall Street analysts are far more ignorant, but wield less direct power).

Some of this retailers have unfairly become the whipping boy for every liberal cause simply because they are big. I have no social bone to pick with them, but I do see them as the General Motors of retail. They are big and they make lots of money, but they do so on sheer momentum, using an outdated philosophy of business. While they tout their vast distribution centres loaded with state of the art technology as a source of pride, I see waste on an epic scale that is most certainly built into the price we all pay in their stores. Their logistics system assures that I can always find what I want on their shelves, assuming I want the same thing that everyone else in America and Europe wants, and the cost of such logistics more than eat up the money they saved by placing their purchase orders in China.

A big retailer in USA tossed the Salvation Army out of their stores last Christmas. This year they led the way to banishing the word "Christmas" and implementing 15% restocking charges (under the apparent assumption that product returns cannot conceivably be their fault) but, this retailer has a Six Sigma program, so drowning in inventory and a knack for new policies that serve no purpose other than to remind customers that shopping at their stores is a privilege are about par for the course.

The hope for Lean in retailing comes from the building products sector, where Home Depot and Lowes are doing battle. You don't read much about whiz bang technology driving Home Depot distribution centres (DC) because they didn't waste their money on such things. They have a few DC's for imported stuff, but the rule for doing business with Home Depot is that manufacturers generally ship directly to stores in box and skid quantities. Most of the purchasing is done regionally, rather than from headquarters. A Home Depot store manager has an 800 number for each supplier that he feels quite free to use any time, any day, to replenish whatever is needed in any quantity needed. Lowes is very big on buying from regional manufacturers.

The retail model will change, of that we can be certain. I doubt that some of the big retailers will lead the change. Their vast profits in the past have created a kaikaku-proof culture. But somewhere out there is the Toyota of retailing, who will very soon emerge from the fog. They will be the retailer who studies Home Depot and Lowes, and the one to learn manufacturing best. They will understand the Internet better. It is too economically sound to not happen.

Chapter 3: Challenges and Opportunities in Retail Sector

Traditionally, the retail industry has been focusing on early technology adoption as a major driver to improve its bottom line. In the 1980's unique packaging codes/barcodes together with point-of-sales systems were implemented to boost efficiency and accuracy. In the 1990's more complex planning tools for forecasting, merchandising, warehousing, distribution, and pricing were introduced to retail operations and finally, in the 2000's cross channel integration, ERP platforms, online stores, and pricing markdown tools were implemented. Still missing until now, are major improvements and investments in inventory management processes between central-warehouse, depots to retail stores/outlets and within retail stores (in-house logistics) itself. While RFID technology and item-level inventory management systems are considered to be technologies to once again drive retailers' bottom line, we believe that these technologies, as with any other technology, extract their full potential only when implemented in combination with a continuous improvement process following and adopting Lean principles ('technology follows process' and not the other way round).

Process and organizational improvement through Lean is capable of addressing most challenges in the retail merchandise life cycle while creating significant and tangible value for retailers through continuous satisfaction and overachievement of customer needs.

There are several trends occurring in the world of retail that pose challenges as well as opportunities for change, such as:

1. Structural Crisis: Revenues of bricks and mortar retail have been stagnating whereas the share of private consumption in this retail channel has been decreasing steadily since the 1990's from 40% share to below 30% today. Another structural crisis has been the eroding margins in that return on sales has been reduced by half in recent years as well.

2. Sub-optimal Price and Product Range Structure: Inefficient price and product range decisions, due to missing/incomplete customer shopping insights.

3. Product Offering not Reflecting Customer Needs: Historically grown/mushroomed product structure, interchangeable products, no customer centric, pro-active, consumption oriented product range management, and increasing complexity costs through unnecessary product range extension.

4. Predominance of Central Procurement: Local market requirements not reflected adequately and customer requirements not reflected sufficiently in prices and product range.

5. Shifting Customer Needs: Revenue potential shifting from bricks and mortar to online retail stores, customers expecting 24/7 availability of information and shopping opportunities, continuously increasing price competency and sensitivity, and soaring diversity in customer segments/segmentation.

6. Private Labels: Declining brand loyalty and increasing revenue share of private label brands.

7. Increased Demand for Lifestyle Products: Increasing degree of customer segment individual products (convenience, organic, etc ...).

8. Life Cycle Acceleration: Product innovations since 1997 increased by 11% annually and flop rate increased in same time from 60% to 69%.

9. Internationalization: Only fast growing retailers with strong home base (customers, processes and organization) achieve decent sales return, and most successful concepts in general are discounters and convenience stores.

Derived from the above-mentioned trends, one of the biggest underlying operational challenges for any retailer has been and continues to be the management of inventory. Finding the Leanest way on how to get merchandise from the factory/supplier to the central warehouse, on to the delivery truck and finally over the outlet backdoor to the shelves is not a simple task. With the application of Lean principles the lead times from factory/suppliers to shelf can be reduced significantly in order to replenish sold merchandise 'just-in-time' and as per customers' expectations, while at the same time improving employees' productivity along the supply chain, achieving accurate inventory levels and reducing out-of-stock situations/lost sales leading to higher revenues and improved profitability. Successful retailers, such as apparel retailer Zara, started implementing Lean in their supply chain first and then rolled it out enterprise-wide making them one of today's most profitable retailers globally.

Lean retail approach Focus Areas

Lean retail approach should focuses on increasing efficiency in core processes by taking on a full supply chain view from as early as planning the season trends all the way to selling the merchandise to the shopper:

1. Sales Planning: Target process setting (KPI's), roles and responsibilities alignment between procurement and disposition, reduction of variants, and definition of optimum merchandise density on shelf.

2. Sales Controlling/Scheduling: Controlling of merchandise (life-cycle management), price reduction/discounting process, and introduction of fire-sales through 'clearing zones.'

3. Logistics: Lead time optimization (factory, supplier to central warehouse and then to depots and outlets), reduction of required warehousing/storage capacity, continuous/just-in-time replenishment, and elimination/reduction of stock-outs.

4. Sales: Freeing up sales clerks' time to serve more customers in better ways.

Areas of waste often identified in a retail environment

1. Transportation and Handling: Unnecessary movement of merchandise, e.g. movement of inventory between one outlet and the other or between outlets and the central warehouse and vice versa, due to customer quality claims (exchanging/returning merchandise) or unforeseen different local market demands for individual product (red product is fast mover in region north, but dead stock in region south).

2. Inventory: Retailers carry more merchandise than necessary. This includes merchandise in transit (e.g. shipment from China) and out of season products that are kept on shelves or in back door storage for several months or even years (though everybody knows that this merchandise in unsellable, even at the highest discount rates).

3. Movement: Unnecessary movement of employees during their work, e.g. customer asking for different size of merchandise and sales clerk has to go to storage room to check and find right size or a warehouse employee walking several hundred meters between racks to pick and kit ordered items for an outlet delivery.

4. Waiting: Delays in previous supply chain steps cause unnecessary waiting for customers, employees or merchandise, e.g. being out-of-stock reflects waiting time for customers, delayed delivery from central warehouse in the morning reflects waiting time for employees waiting at back door to offload merchandise, inventory at warehouses reflects waiting time for merchandise.

5. Over Supply: Supplying merchandise faster than customers' needs, basically supplying it in batches and ahead of demand. Bringing in large quantities of merchandise without matching demand creates excess inventory which results in markdowns and fire sales, which in turn diminishes inventory levels with a negative impact on revenues and profits.

6. Over-processing: Merchandisers inventing the wheel over and over again when setting-up promotional displays and tables rather than sticking to the agreed/pre-defined planogram.

7. Defects: Merchandise in bad quality, merchandise to be reworked, and merchandise that has to be scrapped or sold-off below cost price due to mismatch with customer tastes and requirements.

8. Unused Skills: 60% of sales clerks' working time is tied up with internal house logistics and merchandising tasks, while at the same time customers are wandering around in the store looking unsuccessfully for assistance. Sales clerks' should be focusing on assisting and selling to customers; using their time for anything else is waste.

Chapter 4: Lean Warehousing and Distribution Centre

Over recent years, I have been asked on occasion if you can apply Lean principles to a distribution centre environment. The simple answer is, "yes;" however, applying Lean to a Distribution Centre (DC) is not as straightforward as it is for manufacturing operations. Lean is simply eliminating waste from processes that do not add value and about which your customers don't care harsh, but reality. Lean requires a shift in thinking and approach; hence, "Lean Thinking" requires executive support from the top down.

Seven Wastes

The seven types of waste are outlined below and yes, they do apply to a distribution centre environment.

1. Defects: Wasted effort to create something the customer rejects. This forces added waste management processes; more waste. For example, shipping an incorrect item on an order or the incorrect quantity.

2. Over-processing: Using anything (materials, resources, unwanted features) that is more expensive than needed by the customer. For example, the concept of Lean time replenishment is waste. There is nothing Lean about topping off a forward pick location with unnecessary inventory and allocating resources to complete the tasks.

3. Over-production: More production or acquisition than is needed, generally to hide production problems. The result is excess inventory. Although many distribution centre environments do not actually have manufacturing production processes, many DCs have kitting (single deep bills of material).

4. Inventory: Raw materials, work-in-process or finished goods. If value is not being actively added, even for a small period of time, this is waste. Unfortunately, many distribution centre leaders do not control the actual purchase planning, so they end up managing some amount of dead inventory. It is important that you measure the value of your inventory and report monthly on inventory that is obsolete. A good carrying cost number to use is 12-15%.

5. Inspection: No added value. Waste occurs each time product or an order is inspected. For example, auditing a direct to consumer order prior to shipping is waste. Your goal should be "One Touch, Right Time, First Time."

6. Waiting: Time wasted by workers waiting for resources or waiting for a pull signal. Waiting often leads to additional non-value-add processes to manage that waiting. For example, equipment or employee congestion in an aisle is waste.

7. Motion: of the worker or equipment. Motion that does not add value is waste. As many of you know, travel distance (walking) is the largest labour cost component in a DC. Therefore, a focus should be eliminating unnecessary distance and time moving from location to location (forward pick or reserve locations).

Unlike manufacturing where Lean can be implemented with little to no technology, distribution does require some level of technology.

When considering the steps to make your facility Leaner, reflect on what Peter Drucker once said, "There is nothing so useless as doing efficiently that which should not be done at all." The elimination of waste has been the mantra for manufacturers implementing a Lean program in their operations. Ensuring the highest quality processes resulting in minimal defects or errors is the cornerstone of Lean philosophy. Books have been written, classes taught and certification programs administered tailored to the quest of streamlining production. For those of us that live in a distribution environment, we must look to the principles of Lean or Six Sigma and find areas where they can be applied so that the mission of accurate, on-time and cost competitive distribution of goods can be achieved.

Implementing an automated cross-docking process in the distribution centre would be a low hanging fruit when evaluating potential continuing improvement processes. By definition, cross-docking is the direct flow of goods from receiving to shipping thereby bypassing any of the storage, replenishment, picking or sorting activities while maintaining the value-added function of order consolidation.

In order to put an automated cross-docking system into operation, there are some critical requirements that must be met. Vendors supplying products to your DC must provide advanced shipping notices (ASN) along with appropriate unit labelling, either bar code or RFID. When shipments hit the receiving dock, they can be placed onto a conveyor, scanned, and the products will be validated against the ASN with appropriate routing instructions married to each unit. As a result of having an ASN, the Warehouse Management System (WMS) already knows what to expect the shipment and all of its contents and therefore will have already determined the destination of each unit as it is scanned and received into inventory. Should the unit need to go to storage, then a transaction in the Inventory Management System (IMS) would add the unit to the inventory and the unit would be routed to the proper storage area of the warehouse however, if the unit is flagged to go to shipping and become consolidated into an existing order, then the conveyor would route the unit directly to the outbound shipping sorter.

In addition to vendors providing ASNs and also having the automated material handling system integrated with the WMS in place to support the cross-docking operation, vendors must also understand and provide the proper packaging and labelling to support the outbound shipping processes. Shipping sorters require specific labels in certain locations on the box or carton. The labels must also contain the data needed to support the sortation and order consolidation processes. Also, it is critical for customer satisfaction to partner with vendors and ensure that packaging of goods is consistent with the needs of the distribution centre's customers, whether the customers are consumers or retail stores.

With this basic understanding of an automated cross-docking operation, here are five advantages that should be considered in deciding whether to implement this system in your DC that parallel the principles of both Lean and Six Sigma.

Advantage 1: Reduced Cost per Unit Shipped

Since cross-docking bypasses the put-away, replenishment and order picking processes, the more products your operation can cross-dock, the more labour savings you will recognize. Although every distribution centre is different, even distribution centres for the same company, it can be conservatively estimated that the put-away, replenishment and order picking processes together make up at least 50% of the total warehouse operation expenses. In many cases, the percentage is over 75%.

Now imagine what would happen if you could put systems and processes in place to bypass all of that labour for 50% of your products that you ship with an automated cross-docking operation. By saving 50% of the total warehouse operation expenses for 50% of the products, the result would be a 25% savings in total warehouse operating expense. This savings would have a huge impact on the ever-so-important measurement in distribution centres; cost per unit shipped.

Other areas where the automated cross-docking operation would reduce the cost per unit shipped includes the reduction of effort needed to support the inventory process. Whether the DC does a physical inventory or cycle counting, by eliminating the number of products stored in inventory, the labour needed to ensure inventory accuracy will also be reduced.

Advantage 2: Faster Lead Times to Customers and Retailers

Cost, Quality and Lead Times are typically the three main factors influencing purchasing decisions. Therefore, your company's position compared to your competitors is determined by the performance of each of these factors. In a retail environment, especially during a high demand season, just having an item on the shelf is often enough of the competitive advantage needed to win a sale. "Out of stock" or "backordered" are terms that are rarely met with customer satisfaction, even if the item is scheduled to be restocked on the next day.

An automated cross-docking system is about as close to just-in-time delivery, or delivery-on-demand that a distribution centre can provide their retailers or consumers. To be able to continue to add the value of order consolidation along with improved lead times will ensure that your business is doing its best to provide the highest level of service for these valuable customers.

Advantage 3: Reduced Required Warehouse Space

By eliminating the number of products stored in inventory, the physical infrastructure needed, whether represented by square foot of warehouse space or material handling storage equipment like pallet rack or shelving, is also reduced or recaptured for other purposes.

This reduced square footage is not only beneficial from a real estate perspective, but it also helps improve day to day productivity. The value-added work provided by the warehouse labour staff includes activities such as receiving, put-away, order picking and consolidating. The non value-added work includes travel time. As an example, travel time exists when a warehouse worker has to replenish the order picking module with items pulled from a pallet located in the bulk storage area on the other side of the warehouse. By reducing the travel distance, the warehouse worker spends less time on the non value-added work and therefore improves productivity by being able to accomplish other value-added tasks.

Advantage 4: Better Shipping Accuracy

The term "Six Sigma" originates from the degree of accuracy that processes should aspire to become. In statistical analysis, sigma is the standard deviation of a group of numbers. Six Sigma means that a process should provide acceptable results, results that fall within six standard deviations of the mean, so that there is only 1 defect in 3.4 million attempts.

As it relates to the distribution environment, the cause of errors is almost always a result of a human mistake. In designing new distribution centres or re-engineering existing distribution centres, material handling engineers focus on minimizing the number of touches required to support a specific operation or series of operations. The reason is because each touch poses the risk of an error occurring, even if the probability of the error is small, say 0.05%. That translates to an accuracy of 99.95% which on the surface seems pretty good however, if in the lifetime of a single stock keeping unit (SKU) that travels into and out of a warehouse, it is touched 5 times (receiving, put-away, replenishment, order picking and consolidation), the resulting accuracy is 99.95% multiplied by itself 5 times, which equates to 99.75%.

On the other hand, if utilizing an automated cross-docking operation allows you to bypass the put-away, replenishment and order picking processes and the errors associated with these processes, the SKU is only touched twice which translates into an overall accuracy of 99.95% multiplied by itself twice, which equates to 99.9%. This may appear to be insignificant, but if your distribution centre is shipping 20,000 items a day, the difference between 99.9% accuracy and 99.75% accuracy is 30 less errors and 30 less errors mean 30 less labour intensive returns and restocking activities and 30 less unsatisfied customers.

Advantage 5: Improved Financial Position

An automated cross-docking system can improve your three critical financial statements that are evaluated by your creditors; Profit and Loss Statement, Balance Sheet and Statement of Cash Flows. As previously discussed in Advantage 1 in this chapter, the automated cross-docking system can eliminate a significant portion of the warehouse operating expenses. As a result, either you can reduce your sales price and gain market share or you can maintain your current sales price and gain gross margin. Either way, you are bound to become more profitable.

Because the automated cross-docking system can reduce the required warehouse space, this can translate into reduced leased or purchased square footage in real estate. This reduction will help strengthen the balance sheet because if a square footage would be purchased, you would save on cash (short term asset) by purchasing less real estate or storage equipment (long term assets). If you were to lease the space, you would not have such a large long term liability in the form of the lease. Both scenarios provide stronger balance sheet ratios.

An automated cross-docking process can also be extremely beneficial to the Statement of Cash Flows. The reason is simple; items at rest stored in inventory do not create cash whereas an item in motion flowing efficiently through the distribution centre does create cash. It is easier to think of those boxes that you distribute as being full of your cash, but you cannot take the cash out of the box until it gets loaded onto the truck at the shipping dock. Obviously a process that receives that box and then sends it directly to shipping in order to take the cash out is a better situation than putting that box on a shelf for a day or two before picking it and sending it to the shipping docks.

The benefits of an automated cross-docking system are often far exceeding the costs to put into operation, even when the system is implemented in an existing operation compared to a new facility. The system will provide Lean methods to the distribution process and also help improve inventory and shipping accuracy by eliminating the possibility of errors induced from human touches. All of these improvements can be easily benchmarked and measured for continuous improvements; however, the ultimate measure of success will be the end result; more happy customers.

A Lean warehousing and distribution centre is not built in a day. It requires long-term vision and strategy, and effective use of all the tools and resources you can bring to bear. It isn't easy or even cheap, but it can improve your real, measurable efficiency dramatically, and as overheads continue to shrink, it becomes one of the few valid strategies that will allow growth and prosperity in certain markets.

Your goal is decreased idle inventory levels, better customer fill numbers, better accuracy, and more efficient equipment and personnel utilization. You can imagine some of the problems you will have to solve before you start to realise these goals, but others will escape you. Complete and committed buy-in from all of your key stakeholders is absolutely vital, if you hope to make any real ground.

Toyota was an early adopter of Lean warehousing and distribution processes, and we can learn from their experience

The core of the Toyota Production System, as they called their groundbreaking process, form the core of Lean logistics planning today. It involves universal personnel training and motivation, standardisation of processes and equipment, waste reduction and PDCAC (the Plan, Do, Check, Act Cycle) problem solving processes.

Personnel training must start with recognising that your people are your first chance to identify any problems and craft real practical solutions to them. Make sure all of your people (not just managers or leaders) are aware of your value stream, and how they fit into it. Make sure they know that any activity that does not add value is wasted effort.

Standardisation of your processes is important because it allows for better alignment of your processes to each other, and makes planning for zero waste possible. Standard work is not the goal, but rather a baseline upon which you can build truly elegant and efficient solutions to problems.

In terms of inbound and outbound warehouse flow, you need to embrace the idea of hitting goals exactly. The perfect quantity in the perfect place at the perfect time. Visual management techniques may be helpful in this, because it allows real-time decision making and supports low-inventory flow management.

Chapter 5: Lean Retailing and Inventory Control

A Case Study

Manufacturers of consumer goods are in the hot seat these days. In the past, retailers would place large orders at the beginning of each selling season, and factories would simply produce to order; but the big chain stores are increasingly adopting Lean retailing practices, so they are insisting that manufacturers fill orders to replenish retailers' stock on an ongoing basis because factories usually can't produce goods fast enough to meet these orders, manufacturers often hold large inventories for indefinite periods.

The cost of holding these inventories is growing. Consumers are demanding greater variety in products, and their preferences are getting harder to predict. As products proliferate and become more susceptible to changing whims, the risk grows that a given product line will have disappointing sales and have to be discounted; but if a manufacturer decides to go Lean on inventories, it runs the risk of stock-outs, lost sales, and endangered relationships with the chains.

It is a tough position, but a new approach can help manufacturers predict their inventory needs more accurately. Manufacturers tend to treat every stock keeping unit (SKU) within a product line the same way; but in fact, these SKUs often have very different levels of demand. By differentiating SKUs according to their actual demand patterns, you can reduce inventories on some SKUs and increase them on others thereby improving your profitability for the entire line.

Differentiating SKUs can also help you rethink your sourcing strategy. Instead of producing all the SKUs for a product line at a single location, either offshore at low cost or close to market at a higher cost, you can typically do better by going for a mixed allocation. That way, you can meet the demands of retailers while controlling costs and inventory.

The Inventory Dilemma

To illustrate, let's consider the inventory problems of a hypothetical company called Hindjeans. In the 1980s, this blue-jeans manufacturer offered about 1,000 different SKUs a dozen styles of jeans spread across a few dozen sizes, with total annual sales of 20 million pairs. Each season, Hindjeans built up its inventories in preparation for big shipments to retailers. The inventories were enormous just before the shipment date, but the risk was small because all of those jeans matched actual orders retailers had submitted several months before. Inventory, in fact, was just a means of spreading out the demand so factories could achieve a steady, efficient flow of output. For Hindjeans, the only cost of inventory lay in the working capital tied up there and in the minor expense of the warehouse. The retailers bore the major cost of inventory; the risk that sales would prove disappointing and the jeans would have to be marked down below cost.

Then in the 1990s, partly to minimize this risk, most of Hindjeans's retailers began to adopt Lean retailing practices. They shifted most of their ongoing inventories and risk back to Hindjeans by keeping on-site inventories low and placing weekly replenishment orders. Since the lead time for manufacturing jeans was several weeks, Hindjeans could no longer make to order; it now had to predict the weekly demand for jeans and set production schedules accordingly and even if Hindjeans got the average weekly demand right, it also had to take into account those weeks with unusually large orders. To ensure that it could fill those orders and keep its retail customers happy, Hindjeans had to estimate the weekly variability in demand and hold a safety stock of finished goods in inventory.

That is difficult enough, but product proliferation only made things worse. In the 1980s, most of Hindjeans's 1,000 SKUs garnered fairly high sales. Big volume tended to smooth out the inevitable peaks and valleys of demand. That meant the composite weekly demand was fairly predictable and variability wasn't so great, so the safety stock held in inventories was relatively small.

Today, Hindjeans manufactures far more styles and sizes than before it now offers 30,000 SKUs and while total annual sales have risen to 90 million pairs, average sales per SKU have fallen from 20,000 units to just 3,000 or approximately 60 sales per SKU a week, much lower than the 1980 average of 400 and that is just an average. Popular SKUs register hundreds or even thousands of sales per week, but less popular, highly differentiated items may sell only ten across all retail stores. The smaller the volume of sales for any individual SKU, the more those sales tend to vary each week because there is so much less demand to pool together. That means Hindjeans has to stock a lot more than ten pairs of those slow-selling jeans to meet sudden upsurges in demand or risk angering important customers with stock-outs. For the same overall level of sales, the company now has to hold a much bigger overall inventory.

Chapter 6: Lean Supply Chain

Lean aimed to eliminate various types of waste. They include; overproduction (making items before they are needed); waiting (goods in stasis while waiting for the next process); excess movement when shifting goods from one process to the next; inappropriate processing (that does not add value to the consumer); unnecessary inventory; excess motion (that can also compromise health and safety); and defects that result in rework, scrap or complaints.

Many of these relate directly to manufacturing processes, while others can be associated with general supply of goods.

A Lean supply chain is one that produces or provides only what is needed, when it is needed and where it is needed. This typically has a number of key advantages over traditional supply chain management, including:
1. Supply more tightly linked with demand.
2. Lower inventory risk.
3. Processes that focus specifically on activities that add value for the customer.
4. A greater focus on mistake-proof processes.

This leads to improved availability and customer service at a lower cost. While high-volume manufacturing and retail distribution clearly lend themselves to Lean supply processes, what other sectors could benefit from this methodology?

Luxury retail brands

One sector in particular that could benefit from this approach is the luxury retail brands market.

The word 'fashion' implies change and unpredictability. It is a frenetic and fast-paced business and shares the problems of the majority of the consumer goods sector in that it requires secure, on-time supply and a product that will sell through; but at the high end, there are some specific challenges:
1. With several fashion campaigns a year, product change is frequent and deadlines immovable.
2. Volume is relatively low.
3. Quality cannot be compromised and prices are super-premium.
4. 'Uniqueness' in the marketplace is essential if the product is to retain its premium, luxury status.

These issues have traditionally led to a 'get it at any cost' mindset. In these circumstances, the procurement function usually follows rather than leads, with the internal brand designers calling the shots.

The bastion sectors for Lean supply have been all about high volume and low unit cost, yet these are not the most important features of the luxury retail brands sector. This dictates a different approach from both procurement and the supply community.

One UK-headquartered luxury shoe retailer is a great example of a fashion brand company with some real challenges in respect of it how it controls its inputs, outputs and inventory. Its key aim is maximum flexibility and responsiveness in terms of production mix and volumes. Yet the word 'Lean' is not part of its vocabulary.

The firm's supply chain vice president explains that every year, significant research goes into new products and tanneries to satisfy design requirements. A core set of 30-40 tanneries provides staple and innovative materials, with up to 30 additional tanneries supplying new products. The need for change is greater in the summer season because this involves a more colourful product range.

Keeping input volume aligned with demand is important, since there is significant risk of obsolescence within inventories. This can be tricky with so many new materials introduced each season.

As the company's supply chain VP explains. "We work continuously to reduce lead times and improve supplier responsiveness." Nevertheless, up to 95 per cent of the total cycle time is 'lost' in waiting/queuing within this process. The smoothing of supply and removal of bottlenecks is therefore, clearly essential.

One added challenge is the fact that this operation is often required to work with raw material technical specifications that are far from comprehensive; they instead rely largely on approved product samples and "a lot of trust" in their suppliers. They are working hard to define more meaningful technical specifications for their materials.

Another issue for this sector is the short lifecycle of the product once it has hit the market.

Take the example of Belstaff, a high-end clothing and accessories brand that traces its roots to Staffordshire in the 1920s. It faces the combined challenge of a 16-18 week concept-to-shelf cycle time. Yet, in line with the rest of the fashion sector, the product may only survive at full price in the marketplace for three months.

The company's supply chain director, confirms. "These challenges, combined with the fact that the market requires new range elements in place at least twice a year, mean that certain risks must be taken upstream and throughout the supply chain. Pre-buying commitments are made at various stages in suppliers' production processes in order to meet the demands of this marketplace."

This has required Belstaff to develop 'premium relationships' with fewer suppliers while forging closer internal links between the procurement, supply chain, merchandising and retail functions. This can be an uncomfortable marriage of creativity and practicality, which he describes as "getting the right brain talking to the left brain".

Getting it wrong is expensive; selling at full price, more than 60 per cent of what is produced is often considered a success in this market. This statistic underlines how the waste elimination benefits of a Lean approach could make a huge difference within this sector; yet can also rely on internal relationships.

For the luxury retail brands sector and many others; the optimum solution lies in an approach that focuses on Lean, high-velocity supply that respects the sacred cow of super-premium product quality. The need for on-time, defect-free supply makes the Lean approach more essential here.

Chapter 7: Lean IT in Retail Sector

An increasing number of consumers shop on-line. Some consumers go to stores to see and touch products then quickly comparison shop on their smart phones to purchase the product at another retailer offering a lower price. Customers are also using social websites to determine their purchase decisions. To respond to these changes in consumer behaviour, retailers need to be agile.

Lean Retail, an approach that uses technology and network architectures to reduce costs and enable innovation, can increase a retailer's agility in responding to and shaping the consumer's experience.

Lean Retail makes it faster, easier, and less expensive to deploy services needed by the store operations team, the web team, and customers. Lean Retail gives IT staff more time to respond to the needs of the business.

The Challenge Facing Retail Leaders

There are two hurdles that slow innovation. One is the multiple networks in stores. These are created by point solutions for video displays, video surveillance, and point-of-sale (PoS) systems and their attendant devices, such as Wi-Fi devices and others.

The problem is exacerbated by new point solutions and by different organizations being responsible for different networks. This historic layering of one network upon the next increases lost opportunity and fiscal constraints. It also contributes to the overall problem that in retail, IT staff must often spend more than 80 percent of their time on maintenance.

The second obstacle for retail is in the data centre, where retailers must keep up with changes enabled by cloud computing and new technologies. Legacy systems and processes have evolved over time to create silos of deep knowledge in specific technologies, as well as tools that aren't integrated with each other. Legacy systems and processes keep innovation tethered to outdated practices, with the result that retailers have trouble keeping up with the changing customer landscape and with evolving business requirements.

How Lean Retail Supports Store Operations

Leading retailers create trends and also follow them, data matters to them. Retailers need to try new ideas, see if they work, and find out how and what customers are buying. To execute business decisions, a retailer must account for the multiple ways consumers are making purchases. Given this reliance on data and the need for agility, business decision making in retail can be either empowered or constrained by the underlying technical architecture and network.

Consider some of the following ways in which technology can support the collection of data and the testing of new ideas:

1. Put new digital displays in the stores and measure the response.

2. Place video cameras in critical areas not just to stop theft, but also to observe customer traffic and behaviour.

3. Create websites that focus on specific demographics and product lines.

4. Put tablets into kiosks to give customers information and access to virtual experts.

5. Give associates tablets so that they can access information quickly and so they can speed up checkout.

6. Give managers tablets so they can check planogram compliance and monitor tasks, and so they have access to real-time business intelligence on sales and inventory.

7. Monitor, aggregate, and analyze social media feedback on your stores and your brand.

Using data in this way, retailers can get an edge on the competition and better understand the customer. Lean Retail gives operations ways to innovate, test, validate, and then scale effectively from pilot to production.

How Lean Retail Supports Shoppers

1. Planogram compliance makes the store's visual experience more appealing and makes it easier for customers to find merchandise.

2. Shoppers benefit when retailers combine features of the store and the Internet in either venue.

3. Shoppers benefit from access to virtual experts who can help them make buying decisions in the store or on the web.

4. Shoppers want associates who can enhance the store experience with information at their fingertips.

The Challenges Facing Retail IT

IT is incredibly important in retail, but can be perceived by store operations and management as a hurdle as well as an enabler. Of all the different components in retail, the IT department is the one that gets the greatest advantage and agility from the Lean Retail model. Lean Retail reduces the high percentage of time that IT normally spends on maintenance, giving IT time instead to innovate and to execute.

For IT, the primary benefits of Lean Retail in the stores are faster roll-out of new applications and capabilities, reduced operations expenses enabled by remote management of IT equipment, and reduced costs.

Chapter 8: The Effects of Lean in Retail

In the retail sector, Lean approach improves operational flows. Lean retail encourages manufacturers to produce standard products in accordance with the created (placed) orders from retailers pursuant to the demand of their consumers.

Characteristics of the retail market are; strong competition, shorter product life cycle, longer product development time and high sensitivity of demand. In order to be more competitive and profitable today's retailers operate strategically oriented to lower prices and gain exemption from holding unnecessary stocks. Lean retail is an example of best practices of successful operational strategies which management need to accept to maximize the operating efficiency of the retail process.

Elements of Lean thinking are defining value; identification of value streams and the removal of waste; organizing around flow; responding to pull through the supply chain; the pursuit of perfection.

Toyota Production System is now applied not only in the manufacturing industry but in other industries too, including insurance companies, hospitals, airline maintenance organizations, state agencies, the retail industry and many others.

Similar to the concept of Lean manufacturing, the concept of Lean retail is known by many names such as; Lean logistics, Lean distribution and Lean consumption. Attempt to apply Lean concept in retail is recent it dates from 90s. In this regard, a number of retailers such as Wall Mart, Tesco and IKEA are well known.

Lean is a modern retail operating strategy which requires maximum efficiency coupled with identification and elimination of waste. It requires simple workflow, eliminating the loss of effort, time, materials and motifs. With acceptance of Lean approach managers are able to reduce activities that add no value, directly impact and help prevent the potential problems, and improve global operational flow.

Application of Lean techniques, such as the simple organization of work, using "pull" to drive replenishment, removing bottlenecks throughout the supply chain, eliminating wasted effort, wasted time, wasted materials and wasted motion, contributes directly to improving the overall performance in retail. Lean thinking is transforming the traditional way of a retail business to new and more effective way of managing inventory and customer expectation. In general, the application of Lean approach allows the company to reduce costs, increase efficiency, reduce execution time, reduce waste of all kinds, increase profitability and keep low inventories. It also contributes to customers' satisfaction, improving product quality and increase staff moral.

According to research carried out in practice, quantitatively speaking, the effects of Lean thinking in retail are increased comparable sales by up to 10 percent, reduced labour costs by 10 to 20 percent, reduced inventory by 10 to 30 percent, and stock-outs by 20 to 75 percent. It significantly contributes to improved customer satisfaction. All this, in return, reflects the increased store profitability. For example, the return on equity, as a measure of profitability, increased by 5 to 10 percent; because of the significant economic impact Lean approach is applied in many retail formats (stores), such as grocery stores, specialty, apparel, convenience stores, discount, entertainment, and quick service restaurants.

The core of Lean retail is primarily a commitment to eliminating waste. Similar to the manufacturing sector and following the model of Lean approach, the main types of waste in retail are; excess inventory, product defects, unnecessary motion, redundant employees and a waste of time. Managers in retail can use similar tools and principles for identifying all types of waste to improve their operational efficiency. Lean techniques includes:

1. Simplifying the design of work (organization of individual work process should be such as to provide a high degree of feasibility and possible control, so that it has clear start and finish).

2. The use of withdrawal (pull) to create a replenishment (provided that the supply of goods is fuelled with actual demand of customers, as opposed

to forecasts or anticipated demand, so to keep inventory levels low and free space).

3. Removing the bottlenecks through the supply chain (by eliminating inefficiency with shorter delivery time, lower transport costs and defects, and improving the flow of goods and operational performance)

4. Elimination of waste of effort, time, materials and movement (by identifying the core business values, with the elimination of excess movement, time, materials and labour used in the process).

The effective implementation of Lean approach in retail makes greater cost efficiency, increased worker productivity and less waste of time and effort. This in return significantly affects the improvement of customer satisfaction and store profitability.

Generally speaking, the reduction of unnecessary processes and waste and improving customers' experience is in the heart of modern business today. Lean retail is in line with best practice that contributes to improving productivity and economic performance in the shop. The quality of managing the retail company, store or product category may be, therefore, considered with the help of Lean approach. For example, the study found that there is a similar corporate philosophy of business between Toyota and Seven Eleven Japan (SEJ). Both companies achieve very good business performance, create a unique corporate philosophy and operate globally around the world.

The main objective of the concept of Lean retail is the optimization of not only intra but also inter-organizational (i.e. inter and external) processes. In efficient consumer response (ECR) strategy manufacturers and retailers are trying to optimize product and information flows throughout the value chain, with a starting point; point of sale, and by collecting detailed data on the customer demand.

Effective organizational integration of production and retail greatly facilitates the implementation of ICT (information and communication technologies). The development of information on merchandising and logistics (80s and 90s) has significantly contributed to rationalization and centralization of positive effects.
Optimizing the supply chain means faster response of supply in relation to the actual sale.

Introduction of electronic scanner cash registers (mid 80's) combined with electronic data interchange (EDI) or Internet, provides information on the sale which supply chains forward to manufacturers and their suppliers, altogether contributing to faster reaction related to changes in demand. Bar-coding and electronic tracking, in addition to large investments in rationalization, leads to increased turnover speed in distribution centres and warehouses. Based on the package and bonding product range for one output, we can observe a trend towards the distribution centre with no storage space, where the goods are directly re-sorted and packaged in a process known as cross docking.

The concept of efficient consumer response (ECR) introduces not only the optimization of logistics. Data collection via scanners and cash registers provide information about the buyer's behaviour (who are the buyers, what, when and where they buy?), which can be used as a base to create marketing strategy for new product development for the target group of customers. Retailers and manufacturers are able therefore to effectively adapt to customers' demand range. Retailers can also successfully use collected data for the systematic development of new products with manufacturers or, in the case of private labels, with their own particular group of retailers.

All in all, electronic data interchange (EDI) and quick response (QR) improve relations between retailers and suppliers, allowing retail prices to be reduced by 10%.

Managing Product Categories

Managing product categories adequately links retail and production thus contributing to the improvement of efficiency throughout the value chain and, therefore, overall performance in retail. Managers of product categories in retail companies are responsible for only one product category across the entire value chain, starting with suppliers, or even product design, through logistics and cost planning to final sale.

Application of inventory policy for individual items is more efficient compared to the compound in the realization of profits. Companies Home Depot, Wal-

Mart and many others manage inventory for individual items, thus increasing their profits.

The concept of category management may, however, be in conflict with other management requirements. Problem, in fact, occurs in connection with the purchase of large quantities of the individual product categories in cases when negotiating with manufacturers on terms and price. It, too, occurs in the case of application of policies and strategies of differentiated prices (such as, for example, promotion of special offers) which applies to all not just certain categories of products.

Managing product categories is also incompatible with the management of key customers. Managing key customers is a modern concept of business producers which have been traditionally organized by product and now employ special managers for large customers, who operate in all products for all customers.

In principle, the application of Lean in retail contributes to increased profitability. The concept of Lean retail is considered to be relevant to the basic products because of its forecasting capabilities and where the application of the "just-in-time" supply chain concept is appropriate. It may, however, adversely affect the industry supply chain because of its dependence on customers, what can result in a lower or reduced level of profitability.

In addition to these fundamental problems, producers and retailers often have different interests what causes the problem of efficient control of the value chain. This can best be seen in the example of the brand or private label controlled by the retailer. In many areas the value chain integration organization is developed. It can be greatly contributed with the implementation of the concept of Lean retail, as well as with the concept of efficient consumer response. In the buyer driven model (pull not push) retail plays a central role.

Chapter 9: Lean Consumption

Over the past 20 years, the real price of most consumer goods has fallen worldwide, even as the variety of goods and the range of sales channels offering them have continued to grow. Meanwhile, product quality in the sense of durability and number of delivered defects has steadily improved.

So, if consumers have access to an ever-growing range of products at lower prices, with fewer lemons, and from more formats, why is consumption often so frustrating? Why do we routinely encounter the custom-built computer that refuses to work with the printer, the other computers in the house, and the network software? Why does the simple process of getting the car fixed require countless loops of miscommunication, travel, waiting, and defective repairs? Why does the diligent shopper frequently return from a store stocking thousands of items without having found the one item that was wanted? Why is this tiresome process of consumption backed up by help desks and customer support centres that neither help nor support? In short, why does consumption which should be easy and satisfying require so much time and hassle?

It doesn't have to and shouldn't. Companies may think that they save time and money by off-loading work to customers, making it the customer's problem to get the computer up and running, and wasting the customer's time. In fact, however, the opposite is true. By streamlining the systems for providing goods and services, and making it easier for customers to buy and use them, a growing number of companies are actually lowering costs while saving everyone's time. In the process, these businesses are learning more about their customers, strengthening consumer loyalty, and attracting new customers who defect from less user-friendly competitors.

What these companies are doing has a familiar feel. Just as businesses around the world have embraced the principles of lean production to squeeze inefficiency out of manufacturing processes, these innovative companies are streamlining the processes of consuming. In the early 1990s the term lean production was popularized to describe the ultra-efficient process management of our exemplar firm, Toyota. We believe it is now time to recognize lean consumption as its necessary and inevitable complement.

"But surely," you say, "when it comes to consumption, less can't be more." Actually it can be, for both consumer and provider. Lean consumption isn't about reducing the amount customers buy or the business they bring. Rather, it's about providing the full value that consumers desire from their goods and services, with the greatest efficiency and least pain.

The key word here is "process." Think about consumption not as an isolated moment of decision about purchasing a specific product, but as a continuing process linking many goods and services to solve consumer problems. When a person buys a home computer, for example, this is not a onetime transaction. The individual has embarked on the arduous process of researching, obtaining, integrating, maintaining, upgrading, and, finally, disposing of this purchase. For producers and providers (whether employees, managers, or entrepreneurs), developing lean consumption processes requires determining how to configure linked business activities, especially across firms, to meet customer needs without squandering their own or the consumer's time, effort, and resources.

The way to do this is to tightly integrate and streamline the processes of provision and consumption. The challenge is not simply logistical. Lean consumption requires a fundamental shift in the way retailers, service providers, manufacturers, and suppliers think about the relationship between provision and consumption, and the role their customers play in these processes. It also requires consumers to change the nature of their relationships with the companies they patronize. Customers and providers must start collaborating to minimize total cost and wasted time and to create new value.

That may seem like a doubtful proposition. But some companies along with their customers have started the culture shift that will make lean consumption possible and they are finding that everybody wins.

Chapter 10: Lean in Retail Sector

Retail is a broad sector. The issues and opportunities will not be the same depending on whether you are selling shoes, books, or food. Assume you are running a supermarket chain. Then there are opportunities in the customer interaction within your stores, in the shelf replenishment operations, in the receiving and preparation of the goods, and in all aspects of supply chain management.

On the floor, for example, you might work on the following:
1. Reduce customer waiting times at checkstands.
2. Lay out the shelves on the floor to make the most frequently bought items easily available.
3. Position items that are frequently bought together.
4. If you have delicacy counters, you can work on the kitchen where the items are prepared to increase productivity, reduce spoilage and assure the availability of all items on the floor.

Behind the scenes, there may be opportunities in the flow of goods from trucks to the shelves customers pick from. Trucks deliver in pallets or cases that need to be received, put away, and broken into the totes or display cases for customers. Observation of these operations usually uncovers improvement opportunities.

You may have a distribution centre receiving some or all of your items from suppliers, in which you may be able to do the following:
1. Improve the breakdown between items that are delivered straight to stores or go through the distribution centre.
2. Organize delivery milk runs from the distribution centre to stores.
3. Organize collection milk runs to suppliers.
4. Improve flow and visibility in warehousing or cross-docking operations within the distribution centre.

Then you may pursue further opportunities in the information systems used to run the chain. It sells thousands of items to tens of thousands of individual consumers everyday. There may be opportunities to improve the way this flow of transaction data translates into orders to suppliers, with their attendant consequences. These transaction data also need to be mined for differences in customer behaviour in different locations, trends, or correlations between items. Identifying opportunities is the easy part; changing the organization to take advantage of these opportunities is the hard part. The top management of the chain has to want it for strategic reasons, and to have the determination and perseverance to make it happen. Unlike manufacturing, retail is an area where the most successful innovations in recent decades have come from companies in the US, Amazon, or in Europe, like Auchan or Ikea. To the management of a supermarket chain, these may be more compelling sources of ideas than Toyota.

Chapter 11: Applying Lean Thinking in the Retail Sector

A Process, is a Process, is a Process...regardless of what business environment you are in!

'Lean Thinking', a business excellence philosophy that originated in the manufacturing sector, applies equally well in all other business sectors, though there is very little written about this when it comes to the Retail Industry environment.

There are many differences between manufacturers and retailers, and there are a remarkable number of similarities too. Having worked in both, I can perhaps see how this is true, more so than most.

Even amongst retailers, there are certainly significant differences between the product types and service types that they offer, and the modes of delivery. For example, consider the differences between hair-dressers, supermarkets, clothing stores, hardware stores, news agents, post-offices, restaurants, and car dealerships. Lots of differences...but there are also many commonalities.

Fundamentally, they all have customers, (including 'internal customers'), sales and marketing, purchasing, finance and accounting, payroll, the need to hire and train employees, quality issues, delivery schedules and systems, etcetera. For all companies, a customer is a customer, wherever they are, at every step of the supply chain; and a process is a process. There is always room for improvement in any business. The same way that some hospitals and banks are now turning to the manufacturing sector to proactively learn about Lean methods, and learning new tricks that are old hat in the manufacturing environment, so too, there is an opportunity for the broader retail sector to learn some new tricks.

There will no doubt be the nay-sayers who believe that their retail business is so different that Lean Thinking principles and practices won't apply...and that is fine, because this simply lets their competitors...the early adopters, get further ahead. There is no mandate that says every business must be successful, or even survive.

Darwin's Theory of Evolution applies in business just as it does in biology. The ability to adapt to meet the changing environmental conditions is key to long term survival.

Those that don't embrace the opportunities that new thinking provides, end up being 'reactive' and playing catch-up later. Now is the time for early adopters of Lean Thinking in the retail industry to make the break from the pack.

Most seminars about Lean Thinking and Retail seem to focus on the logistics aspects, including warehousing and wholesaling, rather than what happens at the retail customer interface; but none the less, 'Lean Thinking' principles and practices do apply directly to Retail. Much of the 'business excellence' or 'operational excellence' literature in the retail sector focuses on 'Sales and Marketing' and IT (Information Technology) systems, electronic processing, etcetera. Very little is available when it comes to pure and simple process 'flow' and quality of the day to day business, where real people are involved.

This is an area of opportunity for the Retail sector where smart retailers can attract and retain more customers, thereby increasing revenues, while at the same time reducing their costs and improving the customer's buying experience.

So how does 'Lean Thinking' apply to Retail?

A key tenet of 'Lean Thinking' is to provide 'value' to the customer…where 'value' is defined by the customer…those elements of the product or service that the customer believes they legitimately should be paying for…without paying for un-necessary process waste. Further, this value should be provided at the rate that the customer requires it, when the customer requires it, where the customer wants it, in a smooth, uninterrupted flow.

So let's consider some examples of what we mean by 'value'.

Is it just the 'lowest price'?

Suppose, as a customer, you want to buy a carton of milk, and you are an equal distance from your local supermarket and from your local convenience store, with the only difference being that the milk at the supermarket is cheaper. Where will you go to make your purchase?

If you are in a rush, it's very possible that you will choose the convenience store, and pay a premium, because at that moment, time is 'valuable' to you (as well as the milk), and there is a high probability that you may be waiting in a long queue if you go to the supermarket. So clearly, 'value' isn't always just about the lowest price.

Waiting in a queue is of no value to the customer, and anything that is part of the process that isn't of value, by definition, is 'waste'.

Customers usually value their time, and retailers know it. Campaign promises such as 'if you have to wait more than 5 minutes, then it's free' is an indication of this. If we consider the supermarket example, I can recall years ago where, if you wanted to purchase a single item in a supermarket, you could be in a queue behind a long line of people with grocery trolleys stacked to the brim. To reduce this regular occurrence, supermarkets started introducing specific checkout isles labelled '15 items or less', then '8 items' or less. This is an example of focussing on what the customers value, and then going about giving it to them by improving the flow; a key concept in Lean Thinking. Some stores now have the facility for customers to scan and handle the payment transaction for their products themselves, without the need for a checkout person' to do it for them.

We don't know what we don't know!

Does Lean make sense in Retail?

It makes sense that doctors wash their hands in an antiseptic solution prior to operating, to minimise the risk of infecting the patient. We know it, and it just makes sense. Though until the middle of the 19th century, it didn't make sense to anyone! Doctors just went about their business...business as usual...not washing their hands prior to operating. Even after the evidence was in, there was strong push back from Doctors who didn't like being told they should do things differently...'a better way'. They wanted to stick to their 'comfortable', but archaic practices. All they were being asked to do was wash their hands...it wasn't rocket science (especially since there weren't rocket scientists in those days). Leading and managing change isn't easy!

You may be surprised, or even confronted by the suggestion that many of the everyday 'business as usual' practices in the retail industry are just as archaic, compared with what they could be if Lean Thinking principles and practices were more widely practiced.

Lean Thinking isn't some complex esoteric set of principles and practices it is a simple approach that makes a lot of sense, and provides the promise of a better way, with better results. In hindsight, after a successful implementation, the 'answer' will appear self-evident (as it often does), and we will wonder why we didn't always do it this new, simple way.

I still remember when I was a kid, going into the bank. Instead of a single queue, there used to be a separate queue for each teller. You did walk into the bank and make your way to the queue that appeared shortest, only to find that the other queues were flowing quicker...because the person at the front of your queue had a complex transaction rather than a simple deposit or withdrawal. You did see other customers that came into the bank after you progress forward in another queue and be in and out while you hadn't yet moved; how unfair! Should you change queues? Will the person at the front of your queue be gone any instant...or will they be there another 10 minutes? (Invariably you did always know that jumping queues would work to your detriment, because Murphy's Law is pretty robust.)

These days, all the banks that I know of have a single queue, and when you get to the front of it, you simply wait for the next teller to indicate (often via a light or bell) to let you know that they are ready for you. In Lean Thinking parlance, this is a 'pull system' (sometimes referred to as a kanban system, with the light or bell being the kanban signal) where the bottleneck (i.e., the part of the process that is capacity constrained) is ready for the next piece of work.

In hindsight, this is so simple that it makes me wonder why it wasn't always done this way. I am still wondering why the likes of McDonalds doesn't implement this same, simple and fair approach.

What is in a name?

'Lean Thinking' is an unfortunate term. The 'Lean' bit originally referred to 'trimming the fat' from processes during product manufacture. The name is unfortunate because it often has connotations of being about cutting jobs, or being 'Lean and mean'.

It is actually about doing things sensibly to free up time, remove various forms of waste, and provide a better experience for the customer (and employees), and to become more competitive as a business. The point is, 'Lean Thinking' is about continuous improvement and business excellence. It is not rocket science (though there are those that would like to have you think it is more mysterious than it really is.)

There is also another continuous improvement methodology known as Six Sigma, with its own unfortunate name (unless you are a statistician, where the name becomes suddenly meaningful...but let's not go too far into that discussion). These days, the Six Sigma approach has gravitated toward the Lean approach to the extent that there is now 'Lean-Six Sigma', in an attempt to address the drawbacks of following the pure Six Sigma approach. Having been involved with Six Sigma for quite some time in one of my previous roles in a large international organisation, my view is that Six Sigma is simply an approach, for certain types of problems, beneath the Lean Thinking umbrella. It's not an either/or approach. The point is, don't get too hung up about the name.

Lean is about making things simple, it is not surprising that there is evidence of some Lean Thinking practices and principles having been implemented within various businesses in the retail environment...even though those who have made the improvements may not know there is a 'name' or 'label' for a particular concept they have implemented. The issue is that where this has occurred, in most cases, only certain elements have been applied, and a structured approach is generally not evident...so there is plenty of opportunity left on the table.

McDonalds is one of the retail exceptions, where a structured approach has been taken. The key issue here is that they have a limited range of standardised products, and most retailers don't understand enough about 'process' to learn the lessons that can be learned from McDonalds.

Words of Caution

Beware the nay-sayers!

There are people who will tell you a thousand reasons why Lean won't work in the Retail Industry.

We all know that the earth is round, and that it orbit's the sun...though back in Galileo's day, the general population took a lot of convincing, particularly those in power (i.e. the church) who believed the earth to be the centre of the universe. Galileo had proof to the contrary! That wasn't enough! The saying 'there are none so blind as those who refuse to see' rang true as Galileo was persecuted for his 'heresy' and beliefs.

What it takes, for the truth to be known, is for some open minded influential souls...to become early adopters and blaze the trail for others. 'Seeing is believing' and the competition will inevitably follow.

Lean is simple, but unfortunately, in the majority of applications (even in the manufacturing industry where it is common), it has been implemented poorly. In fact, the 'Lean' label has been used, but the Lean philosophy hasn't been implemented at all. My analogy is a doctor washing his or her hands in dirty water, rather than in an antiseptic solution, prior to operating. Poor or misguided application leads to poor results!

Some banks have made some in-roads in an attempt to apply Lean Thinking principles and practices, though they still have a lot to learn...because their focus is still too much on short-term cost-cutting, and out-sourcing jobs to countries with lower wage rates, rather than improving internal efficiencies and competing on a 'value-based' customer focused basis that delivers them a better bottom-line overall...but that is another story.

True Lean is based on respect for people, and growing your people as well as your business. The Lean tools are only 10% of the story. It is by leveraging your employees' brain-power and willingness to be proactively engaged in continuous improvement, doing the right things, in the right place, at the right time, that delivers sustainable improvement in business results.

For those who seek to use Lean as a way of reducing headcount in the short term to reduce costs, expect that employees will see through this and resist it. Consequently, momentum for real continuous improvement will be short lived, and net beneficial results will be compromised.

A Question to test your perspective.

Why do you want to introduce Lean?

For the majority of private enterprise, a related question is:

What do you want to do as a business?

Save money?

...OR...

Make money?

The successful implementation of Lean as a business strategy is very dependent on leadership's attitude and buy-in. It is not a short-term fix. The way in which the leadership team of your business answers the above question will give an indication as to the likely success of a Lean implementation.

Think about it. Just imagine that by engaging all your employees in continuous improvement it led you to a more competitive position where many of your costs went down (relative to revenues), while customer demand and revenues went up; leading to a better bottom line. You may well find that the expansion of the business requires you to employ more people to keep up with the growth...and if not, natural attrition over a period of time will allow gradual reduction in staff numbers, with employees feeling much more secure about their jobs, and much more engaged in building the business. This is in line with the Lean philosophy.

This is not to say that there is never an argument for reducing staff numbers in business. If you are in a market that becomes virtually redundant (wagon-wheels, typewriters) then you either adapt to new market demands, or shrink. But while there is still market demand, continuous improvement is your best chance of being competitive, capturing market share, and protecting your employees' jobs to the extent possible.

Lean IS SIMPLE...but it's not necessarily EASY, and there are lots of traps for new players. Amongst the traps are misinformation and inconsistent definitions about what Lean and Six Sigma are; and the common assumption that Lean is just a set of tools.

Don't be put off by this because the potential rewards are great (including from an environmental sustainability perspective). Just proceed with caution. My recommendation is to get yourself a trusted advisor who knows what they are talking about. That is one of the most critical parts, and perhaps the most difficult, since without some expertise in the area, how do you make the right choice? If you get the wrong advisor, expect that you will get plenty of hype and talk about 'tools'. The Lean tools are necessary, but totally insufficient on their own.

The starting point should not be about the tools, but rather, as a business, what is the key problem you are trying to solve…what is driving your need for change? As a company, where are you now, and where do you want to be? Let's not start driving until we know where we want to go.

Be aware that Change Management plays a critical role in any improvement process, and getting this right is a critical element of your success.

Chapter 12: Effective Retail Manager

As many retail managers have come at their profession from a vocational angle, few have degrees in management, meaning many learn on the job.

While this is a great way to get to grips with the nuances of a particular retail organization, it can have its pitfalls, as much of the route to expertise will require plenty of trial and improvement.

So, which challenges are likely to be most important for a retail manager, and how best can they be overcome?

Here is our suggestions on becoming an effective retail manager.

What should a retail manager do?

Retail managers, in the simplest terms, are necessary to increase and maintain a steady stream of productivity across a retail environment. Though this may sound simple, it requires a skill-set that covers four broad areas as follows:
1. Time management.
2. Recruitment and supervision of staff.
3. Facilitating and maintaining changes.
4. Staff motivation, moral and effectiveness.

Now that we have identified the areas in which effective retail managers must function as experts, let's take a closer look at the ins and outs of each area.

1. Time management

In some respects, it can be easy to neglect time management when approaching a retail manager role. This is because you cannot create time like magic; it's a finite resource, and when it's gone, there is little you can do about it.

Time management, then, requires a skilled retail manager to follow these suggested general rules:
    a. Don't let the urgent necessarily take priority over the important. Problems will arise unexpectedly, but knowing when they should be dealt with immediately at the potential detriment of other tasks is part of being a skilled manager. Delegation is your friend here.
    b. Identify and deal with time wasters, including sloppy staff and inefficient processes.
    c. Don't be afraid to say no. If you can't do something, you can't do it. Being a "yes" man is not a virtue.

2. Recruitment and supervision of staff

As a retail manager, ultimately, your potential only stretches as far as that of your team. The key to successful staff management is trust. Trust them to manage themselves and provide them with incentives to work hard, and you may be pleasantly surprised.

You could:
a. Implement mutual evaluation protocols on a regular basis.
b. Set clear, achievable goals.
c. Encourage communication across all platforms.
d. Lead regular training sessions.

3. Facilitating and Maintaining changes

When it comes to retail, change shouldn't just be expected, it should be anticipated and prepared for.

Here is how to both facilitate and maintain change in a fast-moving market and to implement a culture of adaptation across your organization.
a. Forecast change where possible.
b. Manage team efforts.
c. Eliminate a resistance to change by associating it with improvement.
d. Keep everyone informed.

4. Staff motivation, moral and effectiveness

Staff motivation is the key to successful management and maintaining it should be an ongoing priority not something you attempt to build in one fell swoop before announcing the job to be complete. You must continually work toward staff satisfaction. Here are a few ways to do so:
a. Make goals group-based.
b. Encourage teamwork.
c. Delegate responsibility to demonstrate trust.
d. Treat all team members equally.

e. Utilize cross-training programs.
f. Formalize procedures for team feedback.

If you need help with your Lean initiative, contact AA Global Sourcing Ltd. www.aaglobalsourcing.com We offer a variety of Lean programs to suit your needs.

Chapter 13: Using Lean in Retail Stores

Tracking of flow in a retail store

In a retail store, the concept of tracking material flow through the process can be difficult. It's harder to stand in a store and watch material flow like you can on the warehouse floor.

Products and services do flow; you just need to use tools like a Value Stream Map and Customer journeys to see it. Start with the customer and go all the way back to your supplier.

Tradition of individuality

People who work in store areas particularly are given some guidelines or an overview of how the work should be performed, but they are generally left to their own devices to structure the daily tasks. This individual control over work can lead to resistance to defining processes in their areas. People fear losing whatever creativity and freedom they have in being able to do their job any way they see fit.

The only way to get your people to accept process change easily is to involve them in deciding what has to change and how. Include them in the creation of best practices, preferred methods, standards and on your Lean team.

Learning how to recognize waste

Retailers in general have not been trained to observe their processes to identify the eight types of waste. Start viewing your business using the Lean waste filter. You will be amazed at what you will see.

Lean terminology can be intimidating

Simplify and conform Lean terminology and methods to match your current terminology. You already have your own culture and terminology so translate Lean to your terminology when possible. You will gain traction faster.

Lack of meaningful data and lack of data-based decision-making

Know how long the queue is, how long on average it takes to service a customer, and how long it takes to unload a trailer.

Lack of data requires additional time spent gathering baseline data and metrics. You need the data to make informed decisions based on facts.

People can't be controlled like machines

People are your major assets, but they are also your major cause of variation and can resist the change imposed on them. You must pay particular attention to people issues at the beginning of a project; this is achieved by including people working in the area on the Lean team or Kaizen event.

There is always a great amount of variability in every aspect of retailing (e.g., sales forecasting, inventory control, task management, etc.)

With Lean, you need to identify the variability in your business and then use the Lean toolbox to reduce the variability. This will help drive down cost. At a store, this may mean trailer shipments that can be processed with the same size staff.

Increase your flexibility when variability cannot be reduced. In stores, this could translate to cross training employees.

Complexity exacts an enormous costs on store processes

You need to focus on standardizing components and sub processes as much as possible. This will really help reduce process and service complexity. Use the "KISS" principle (Keep it Simple Stupid) when developing your Preferred Methods.

Use a Kaizen event and Lean teams to identify opportunities and then develop solutions

A Kaizen will use common sense to improve cost, quality, delivery and responsiveness to your customer's needs. A Kaizen is a one-week event that uses small cross-functional teams aimed at improving a process or problem identified within a specific area in a very short period of time ("Quick Wins").

A Lean team should be set up to drive continuous improvements in an area that is more complex than a Kaizen event can solve.

Improvements in productivity are based upon

Best Practices: The optimal material flow strategy and equipment to meet customer demand.

Preferred Methods: The optimal way to perform an individual task.

Standards: Develop the engineering standards for each of the work methods that feed your labour allocation and scheduling system.

Poor methods or processes should not be optimized.

Chapter 14: Using Lean to Reduce Employee Turnover

Is Your Retail Workforce a Revolving Door?

From the loading dock to the warehouse floor to the retail store, your workforce is a critical link in your supply chain. It can also have a powerful impact on customer service, efficiency and your bottom line, especially when you have to ramp up or down to keep up with demand. Hire too many workers and you run the risk of unnecessary costs. Hire too few and you could face delays, downtime or overtime.

Meanwhile, another issue compounds the problem; employee turnover. It's a persistent problem that plagues all-too-many retail operations. Recruiting, hiring and training new employees can be costly and time-consuming. Fortunately, with a Lean Labour Management strategy, you can open the door to a more flexible, productive and motivated workforce and close the door on employee turnover.

Companies that implement Lean Labour Management typically see measurable improvements; ongoing savings, an improved ability to attract and retain quality workers, and better use of capacity, to name a few.

So, how do you put Lean Labour Management to work for your retail supply chain?

Five Tips for Putting Lean Labour Management Practices to Work

Consider these five tips to get more from your workforce investment by focusing on your people.

1. Cultivate a Lean Culture

Whatever business you are in, the direct route to delivering long-term customer value and outstanding business performance is a Lean culture. Rooted in Lean manufacturing, Lean labour management improves efficiency by standardizing tasks, processes and the use of technology/materials handling systems. It also harnesses the power of any organization's most valuable resource; its people.

So what does a Lean organization look like?

It creates value by eliminating waste. If a process doesn't add value for a customer, it's eliminated. Lean motivates staff to continuously improve and solve problems with tools like Kaizen, value-stream mapping, and root-cause analysis. Standardized work processes map the right practices to improve performance and train and cross-train employees. Visual tools like boards and TV screens engage employees to lower costs, improve quality and reduce lead times. More important, a Lean operation has rewards in place to keep the work flowing. By "going Lean", retailers can set performance goals and reward employees for exceeding them; both essential to retaining staff.

2. Empower your people by engaging them at every level

The concept of People Involvement is at the heart of Lean Labour Management. In fact, it's the most important of the five Lean Guiding Principles. In a Lean environment, employees work together as one team and are encouraged to root out waste, eliminate problems and make improvements. Lean employees persist when confronted with difficulties, are proactive, take personal initiative, understand what is important and take appropriate action and are deeply engaged with the organization.

So how do you "deeply engage" employees to foster loyalty and prevent turnover?

You empower them by creating an atmosphere of mutual trust and respect. You let them know they are valuable assets whose ideas are vital to the company's success. You communicate company goals and strategies, train and cross-train and provide the tools and encouragement workers need to be effective in their jobs.

3. Set up a positive feedback loop

One of the best ways to prevent great employees from walking out of the door and motivating all employees to give their best is by rewarding them. In a Lean organization, employees are recognized and rewarded for making suggestions that add value. Supervisors make sure their teams understand how their work contributes to the company's success.

Visual cues and job aids encourage employees to "get it right the first time" and when they do, they are rewarded for their efforts.

Effective rewards programs deliver ongoing value and performance improvements, whether the reward is a simple "thank you" for a great suggestion, an incentive-based pay program or material rewards like cash incentives and gift cards. By rewarding employees in any of these ways, you don't just reinforce positive behaviour you provide a role model for under-performing employees to follow.

When negative feedback is unavoidable, it's best to frame it as coaching. Instead of singling out an employee in front of peers, present the situation and feedback as an opportunity for the team to improve.

4. Optimize your workforce

Creating an employee-centred culture is essential to preventing employee turnover. So are incentives and rewards. In addition to motivating, empowering and retaining staff, optimizing your workforce helps optimize the customer experience. A Lean Labour Management strategy can help you.
    a. Staff the right number and types of employees by leveraging effective, expert workforce planning.
    b. Train and develop employees to add value to every step and process.
    c. Build a flexible labour pool with cross-trained employees and temporary resources.

5. Get labour practices in line and lower asset costs

If you are responsible for workforce planning, one of the toughest challenges you face is balancing the need for more manpower with pressure to reduce costs.

Take steps to lower costs by:
   a. Rightsizing your workforce to improve utilization of material handling equipment and technology.
   b. Reducing capital investments in equipment and employee supplies (goggles, safety vests, etc.)
   c. Reducing product handling costs and damage by identifying and eliminating ineffective processes.

Could a few strategic changes in your approach to labour management; including people involvement help you prevent employee turnover and optimize your workforce?

Chapter 15: Reducing Cost and Optimizing Service

In these cash-strapped times deep and sustainable cost cutting is the name of the game. We will looks at how retailers can trim the fat without their service suffering in this chapter.

The sound of axes being wielded can be heard in retail businesses across the board. Retailers are a cost conscious breed by nature, but as sales continue to slide extensive cost reduction programmes are in full force; however, that doesn't mean this is a time for panic. Blindly slashing costs with no regard for its impact on customers is a dangerous game.

Furthermore, while many retailers are already focusing on the obvious savings such as labour costs, travel and expenses, they are overlooking a host of other areas of the business in which millions of wasted pounds are slipping through their fingers. As a friend of mine says; "Retailers are taking a fairly functional view to where the cost savings are. Often, they don't go far enough, deep enough or quick enough."

He believes retailers' cost-cutting measures need to be "deeper and sustainable". He adds; "The days of simply introducing compulsory double-sided photocopying are long gone. Senior management need to identify an audacious goal that requires people to demonstrate a real step change in behaviour."

The followings are our suggestions on ways retailers can make their businesses Leaner and recoup some of the wasted and much needed cash that is pouring down the drain. After all, in the present climate, they need every penny they can lay their hands on.

1. Create a cost-reduction culture

There is no point wracking your brains at head office to find ways to make your business run more Leanly unless everyone else in the company is aware of the pressure the business is under. At Staples for instance, profit and loss figures are widely circulated around the business so that everyone is aware of current trading.

It's about clarity. It's critical that the right people are getting the right information and acting on it. Staples also ensures its entire board communicates regularly with general managers and that they spend maximum time in stores, talking to employees throughout the business.

You can never under-communicate. Creating awareness throughout the business is very difficult and you have to consistently drive that message, but it really does make a difference.

Cost cutting also requires consistence; it's no good making cuts at store level but not at head office, because it won't result in the buy-in of the entire workforce.

2. Amend delivery times

Retailers often set up their logistics platforms for timed deliveries to stores, ensuring they arrive at quieter times. They can then time a delivery to fit in with the presence of any extra staff needed to handle the additional workload created however, timed deliveries come with a premium cost attached to them.

At a major retailer we use to work with, a cost-cutting measure suggested by its store managers was to receive stock deliveries at any time. The Company's Chief operating officer says it does mean that if deliveries arrive at busy times it can interrupt service, "but that is where staff have helped us to smooth out replenishment by restocking in quick tranches when the store has down time, rather than bring in extra staff just for deliveries". He says the cost savings are about £40 a store per delivery day. It might not be applicable for stores in shopping centres, which often stipulate timed deliveries to avoid all the trucks arriving at once, but it is certainly feasible elsewhere.

3. Improve price promotions

There is significant scope to ensure retailers' promotional budgets are more wisely spent, so they get the same sales uplifts from a lower spend or generate a higher sales uplift by spending the same. Invariably, retailers run promotions on gut instinct. Sometimes this works, sometimes it doesn't particularly if they buy extra stock to support the promotion but end up with a heap of unsold inventory.

There is a lot to be said for using a more scientific approach, particularly given that cut-price product offers are a top priority for consumers at the moment. You need to look back at historical trends to say; 'By taking X down in price, we got X back in return'. Often, price promotions tend to be a knee-jerk reaction to offload excess stock but right now retailers need to make sure they have a good fact base of what promotions they have used, the lessons learnt and some view of the qualification of results.

4. Stop wasting time

Retail businesses are notoriously unwieldy, leading to endless hours of wasted time as the numerous departments from merchandising to logistics to IT attempt (and invariably fail) to communicate with each other. The problem is that wasted time is never viewed as a real cost to the business. In our view, it's one of the two biggest costs.

We estimates that as much as 30 to 40 per cent of people's time is spent dealing with internal friction. We advises retail chief executives to go down through the layers of the business and stop listening to those who are telling them what they want to hear. They need to sit in those departments and find out exactly what is getting in the way of helping people do their jobs. If you are a business turning over £100 million and your wages and salary costs are £18 million, if you save 20 per cent in wasted time that is a saving of £4 million.

5. Analyse online information flow

Bricks-and-mortar retailers that have branched out with the launch of a transactional web site are notorious for having gaping holes in the efficiency of their information systems. Many have simply bolted on systems for their online operations. We have spoken to retailers with some really dreadful examples. In order to get details from the web system to the warehouse system some have actually had to pay people to manually type in even basic data such as address details.

Retailers need to look at how information can flow seamlessly from the customer right through to the warehouse. Improved internal processes not only reduce costs in the near term because there will be fewer customer phone calls or e-mails chasing their order and fewer mistakes, but they also potentially increase revenue because customers recommend your service. Time between receipt of online order and the order physically departing should be 15 minutes.

6. Reduce waste

The green agenda isn't just about boosting your reputation for corporate social responsibility; there are major savings to be made by focusing on cutting wastage. One of the many areas where there is a huge amount of excess is transient packaging used to deliver goods to stores. With landfill taxes set to rise in the near future, wastage is costly. Retailers need to liaise with suppliers to work out where packaging could be reduced.

7. Change the way products are shipped

Usually, different products are stacked on separate pallets, picked in the distribution centre then sorted for the shop floor by store staff. Asda in the UK is doing things differently. With its seasonal categories, picking begins in the Far East where labour is cheaper and products are loaded onto pallets according to how they are merchandised in stores.

General merchandising Director explains; "We work out exactly what is going into an area of the store; say Christmas trees, lights, and so on and put them on a pallet together. That goes straight to the distribution centre without picking, so on the same day it's receipted it can go straight out to the store and straight onto the shop floor. This will leads to substantial savings on handling time and frees up storage space. It is complex you have got to decide way in advance what is going where in the store and you need 100 per cent accuracy in the Far East, and once you have decided, you can't change anything. but the savings are worth it. You can all work harder, but you have got to work smarter."

8. Analyse recruitment spend

Obtaining precise figures for recruitment agency spend within large retail organisations is very difficult because countless people across the business are working with agencies it means increased expenditure on administration and a reduced opportunity to reduce that spend. People at head office may think they have got a big handle on it, but it tends to cross so many different parts of the business. Local depots also work with many local agencies, which makes the costs even more difficult to ascertain. Moreover, agencies often increase their prices because they are asked to supply extra staff at the last minute.

Retailers need to start by renegotiating and standardising both pay and charge rates before staff placements start and set specific rules for overtime charges. Potential cost savings are significant.

Chapter 16: Lean Retail is About Time and Money

Lean thinking is spreading in a variety of manufacturing sectors, including consumer goods, apparel, and food and beverage. forward thinking retailers are dramatically changing how products are ordered, moving inventory rapidly through their distribution centres to stores by gathering and sharing point-of-sale data with suppliers, and using bar codes to manage and accelerate product flow.

Although this revolution has been occurring in manufacturing, and for a select few large retailers, most retailers and wholesalers have implemented Lean concepts only minimally if at all and most of those activities have focused on suppliers upstream, rather than on identifying what adds value for customers.

Lean opportunities for retailers and wholesalers fall into three primary categories

1. Retail strategy: For Lean to be successful in a retail or wholesale organization, departmental strategies must align with and support a company-wide Lean strategy.

2. Merchandise management: This involves developing, securing, pricing, supporting and communicating the retailer's merchandise offering. Ultimately, it means having the right product at the right price and the right time. Failing to manage merchandise using Lean principles creates a great deal of waste which doesn't add value for anyone.

3. Store and distribution operations: This is the greatest area of waste and therefore the greatest opportunity to apply Lean principles. Distribution is all about optimizing the trade-offs between handling costs and warehousing costs, and maximizing the warehouse's total cube utilizing its full volume, while maintaining low materials handling costs and minimizing travel time.

More in Store

When seeking Lean improvements in the retail environment, it helps to consider store operations and process improvement from the customers' viewpoint as they make their way through the store. Many companies find analyzing in-store logistics beneficial when it comes to Lean; especially the "last 10 yards" of the supply chain, which encompasses the store's materials receiving process through product selection by the consumer. Much can go wrong during that time from an employee productivity and quality standpoint, and, as a result, many opportunities exist to improve processes and increase profits.

Adding to the complexity of retailer supply chain and operations management is the emergence of multi-channel marketing, which uses brick-and-mortar, online, mobile, and mobile app stores; and catalogue, television, radio, direct mail, and telephone sales to reach the customer. The forms of transactions that result can include browsing, buying, returning, and pre and post-sale service.

Lean thinking is all about identifying and eliminating waste from the viewpoint of the consumer. In these tough economic times, it makes sense to apply these concepts and tools in the retail and wholesale environment, which is as close to the final customer as you can get.

Chapter 17: Tips for Optimising Your Return

There are a lot the retail sector can learn from manufacturing in remaining competitive during challenging times. Retailers should use a set of business improvement techniques under the banner of 'Lean', which aim to streamline processes, eliminate waste and help to focus on quality, cost and delivery. Having worked with over 10 companies in this sector over a number of years, I believe there are opportunities for significant cost savings. Retail does not have a strong track record in utilising process improvement techniques and so has overlooked some very quick and easy 'wins' that could be the difference between profit and loss in a challenging economic environment.

In summary, our top 10 tips are as follows:

1. Engage with staff to work through all internal processes and then together challenge all activities and look to eliminate wasteful practices.

2. Make reducing stock levels a key focus of all staff looking at every stock item; calculate the stock turnover and make every product justify its shelf space!.

3. Make better use of IT and existing computer systems. It's hard to believe how many retailers still use pen, paper and faxes to re-order stock even

though they have the capability to generate electronic orders on their existing systems.

4. Map out the customer journey with staff involvement and look for ways of improving the customer experience.

5. Share the crisis! Introduce visual management boards that display to staff key metrics of the performance of the business e.g. stock turns, sales per employee, average basket spend, sales per sq. metre, etc..

6. Hold regular briefings with staff on these key metrics and talk through the trends and what actions can be done to improve them.

7. Carry out joint improvement activities with suppliers to process map all activities from ordering through to the supply of goods to the retailer.

8. Work with suppliers to get the right quality of goods and correct paperwork.

9. Reclaim store room space and convert it into retail space remember, warehousing space is dead space!

10. Use downtime to provide training for staff and problem solving activities to be ready for the improved trading conditions. Despite the current economic constraints, there is still some funding available in the UK to companies to help them cover the costs of training staff in Lean in order to generate productivity improvements for retailers.

Chapter 18: Making Fashion Retailers More Sustainable

The operating environment for the fashion retailers in India is only moving towards a more challenging and competitive direction even though the market is yet to mature. The market has grown over the last two decades on account of brand proliferation and developing retail network and more recently due to new product category creations. High consumer awareness and exposure to international trends has cut the product life cycles short. Topping this up, the last few years has witnessed the growth of the online platform offering an alternate, convenient and cost effective shopping option for consumers.

It is necessary that fashion retailers manage their operations efficiently both in terms of managing a complex and responsive supply chain at the back end and delighting the customers at the store with great product offers and customer service. Adopting Lean practices can help fashion retailers to achieve significant improvements in store profitability and customer satisfaction, making their retail business sustainable through a positive impact on bottom-line.

The concept of Lean philosophy, pioneered by Toyota, is built on the premise that inventory hides problems. The basic tenet of this philosophy is that keeping the inventory low will highlight the problems that can be dealt with and fixed immediately instead of maintaining inventory in anticipation of any bottlenecks.

"Lean retailing" is an emerging concept and has already been adopted by retail organisations in the Western countries using technology such as barcodes, RFID (across the product value chain from raw material sourcing through production through final delivery at the retail store) and item-level inventory management and network architectures.

In an ideal scenario a retail organization would be Lean at both the store and the distribution centre. The organization would leverage technology such as RFID to uniquely identify the movement of its inventory accurately and use fulfilment logic as per the store's merchandizing principle to have replenishments in tune with customer demand.

Some retailers that have adopted Lean retailing techniques include Wal-Mart, Macy's, Bloomingdale's, The Gap and J. C. Penny. Applying Lean philosophy to fashion retail in India may sound like an 'avante garde' concept as of now however, there are some leading large retailers in India such as the Future Group who are early adopters and have already adopted Lean practices in their retail supply chain.

An understanding of what Lean retailing is and some of its principles can help in appreciating how this concept can make the apparel retail business more sustainable. Lean retailing aims to continuously eliminate "waste" from the retail value chain, waste being defined as any activity/process that is not of "value" to the customer. A fundamental principle of Lean retail is to identify customers and define the "value" as those elements of products or service that the customer believes he should be paying for, not necessarily those that add value to the product. Further the value should be delivered to the customer "first-time right every time" so that waste is minimized.

Lean retailing requires simplifying the workflow design in delivering products to customer. Given that the connotation of value is customer-centric, simplifying the workflow design requires streamlining the core and associated processes so that any kind of waste is eliminated. Further pull-system drives replenishment at the stores (and the shelf) based on what customers want "just-in-time" (neither before nor after the time customer demands). This results in a value flow as pulled by the customer.

Those practising Lean retail have invested in information technology that allows the stores to share sales data in real time with their suppliers. New orders for a given product maybe automatically placed with the supplier as soon as an item is scanned at the check-out counter (subject to minimum order size criteria). Smaller stores may use visual systems wherein the sales staff can gauge through the empty shelf space the products that have been sold and that need to be re-ordered.

Removing bottlenecks throughout the supply chain is another principle driving Lean retail. It entails redesigning processes to eliminate activities that prevent the free flow of products to the customer. Further, Lean retail requires following a culture of continuous improvement. Continuous improvement (or "Kaizen") focuses on small improvements across the value chain that rolls up into significant improvements at an overall level. Kaizens not only can lead to elimination of wasted effort, time, materials, and motion but also focus on bringing in innovations that lead to things being done faster, better, cheaper and easier. Involvement of staff at the lowest levels is very important in Kaizen activities and that means that companies must invest in training, up-skilling their talent pool in Lean Principles.

In the context of apparel retail business, Lean retail can help in improving organizational responsiveness to customer needs, the speed with which the products are delivered to them and meet their expectations as per the latest trends. Systematic application of Lean principles translates in increased throughput (Sales), with lower Work in Process (Investments) and as per customer requirements of Quality, Design, Trends and Time. Improved information visibility across the chain leads to reduced instances of out of stock and excess inventory at the same time, minimizing inventory control costs and reducing shrinkage. At the front-end Lean retail may lead to redesigned in-store processes and systems for consistency in frontline behaviours to provide standard customer experience.

With the focus on training and involvement of the workforce, Lean principles have resulted in improving employee satisfaction without increasing labour costs that in turn positively impacts revenues and profitability. Some retailers in the Europe and USA have reported reducing their store labour costs by 10-20 percent, inventory costs by 10-30 percent, and costs associated with stock outs by 20-75 percent on account of Lean retail.

In addition to top-line and bottom-line impact, Lean retailing by enhancing the enthusiasm and motivation of the frontline staff creates distinctive shopping experiences for customers.

Zara one of the world's largest clothing retailer, has successfully achieved supply chain excellence following Lean principles. It targets fashion conscious young women and is able to spot trends as they emerge and deliver new products to stores quickly thereby establishing its position as the leading fast fashion retailer. The product development processes is based on customer pull-system. Its design team reviews the sales and inventory reports on a daily basis to identify what is selling and what is not. Additionally, regular visits to the field provide insights into the customers' perceptions that can never be captured in the sales and inventory reports. Critical information about customer feedback is widely shared by store managers, buyers, merchandisers, designers and the production team in an open plan office at the company's headquarters. Frequent, real time discussions and interactions within the team help them to understand the market situation and identify trends and opportunities.

Further, Zara manufactures the products in small lots and many styles are typically not repeated. Style cues for replenishments are derived from real time customer demand. At the back end, Zara holds inventory of raw materials and unfinished goods with its supply partners which may be local or offshore manufacturers. Typically, the fashion merchandise is produced at the local manufacturing base and quickly delivered while the staple low-variation range is produced offshore at cheaper costs.

Following Lean retail practices implies a higher stock turn and frequent replenishments by the suppliers based on real-time sales. Building and maintaining reliable and responsive suppliers through win-win partnerships, is imperative to realize the success of Lean retail implementation as high stock turns and frequent replenishments involves the commitment and involvement of the entire supplier base.

Like in any transformational effort, change management plays a critical role in reaping the benefits of Lean retail. The whole philosophy requires paradigm shift in attitudes, behaviours and mind sets of those involved upstream and downstream across the value chain. Training, communicating and inspiring the front end staff is thus an important aspect in the overall success and companies need to device a compelling vision that is shared by employees across functions and hierarchy across the entire chain.

Chapter 19: Retail Values for Lean Leadership

An excellent visual control and reminder to the staff of a local independent bookstore says.

- Talk to everyone.
- Greet everyone who comes through the door.
- Be out on the floor.
- Get to know the books!!

There are strong correlations between retail values and those of lean leadership. The word "retail" comes from the Old French word retailer meaning to cut off, to clip, to pare, to divide, etc. as in tailoring a piece of clothing. Built into the history and identify of retail is to tailor; make a product fit just right for the customer. Lean thinking also promotes customer focused tailored delivery of goods and services; just right amount, timing and quality.

Retail invites an intimacy with the customer unlike that of other parts of the consumption; supply chain such as manufacturing, distribution or wholesale. There is a moment of truth every hour and everyday with customers in retail. The same can be said of any customer facing personal or professional service, but the competition in retail is generally more fierce because the purchase decision is less relationship-based and more price and service-based in retail. The rise of hyper-markets, warehouse stores and internet shopping has changed retail, but it also made strong retail values and behaviours such as those in the visual control above essential for survival of the independent shop.

A successful lean leader must also have this retail mindset; a keen sense of customer intimacy and always being in the moment of truth to deliver a quality product or service. Definitions of lean always being with some form of "customer focus". Yet the customer experience aspect is perhaps one of the least developed areas within lean thinking. We can attribute this partially to the "sales v. operations" culture that exists in many organizations; however just as operations executives should spend time learning on the shop floor or engineering floor, business leaders should spend time learning on the retail floor.

A partial list of "retail values for lean leadership".

- Be out on the floor.
- Be intimate with your customers.
- Know your products.
- Sell right now.
- Sell in small quantities.
- Make time for customers.
- Have can-do attitude.
- Make it right.

An idea central to TQM, kaizen and lean comes to us from Dr. Deming the internal customer. Lean leaders need to practice these same retail values within the organization to sell change, engagement and energetic commitment to each other and the end customers.

Chapter 20: Building a Lean Culture in Retail Distribution Operation

This is a story about an automotive supplier that was teetering on the brink of collapse. When market conditions and customer demand changed, the company lacked the supply chain flexibility or infrastructure to adapt and overloaded its distribution centre with more product lines than it could handle.

Soon, the automotive parts supplier saw complaints reach epic proportions. Unable to address increasing complexity and volumes, the previously stable operation became unstable and unprofitable. As it did, safety, service, and cash reserves plunged.

We came-in to partner with the company in turning things around. Step one was to triage the situation before things spun out of control. Once we stabilized the operation, we could focus on helping the retail supplier get on the road to Lean.

Destination Lean; new leadership, systems and processes

For the retail customer, the second phase of the transformation was to cultivate a Lean culture. This effort focused on three primary goals:
1. Create an incident-free workplace.
2. Improve customer service.

3. Eliminate waste by empowering employees, improving continuously and engaging leadership.

The secret to achieving these goals is by reinforcing the staff with new operations and engineering managers experienced in Lean principles and continuous improvement, and educating high potential managers on Lean. This enabled the company to focus on aligning information systems, standardizing work processes and building a Lean culture.

The new team swung into action, implementing 10 process improvements.

1. Set up more efficient systems for collecting information from the field.

The first step was to set up a system for collecting information from the field. We implemented Management for Daily Improvement (MDI) information centres, comprising whiteboards at GEMBA (on the warehouse floor). The team listed all field failures on the white boards, from inventory overages, shortages or damage to pallets that were either missing or sent to the wrong customer. Next, the team prioritized failures based on the severity of their impacts on customers.

2. Tracked Key Performance Indicators (KPIs) on a glass wall.

To address issues with safety, inventory and quality, the team began tracking KPIs on a glass wall. This included measuring OSHA Recordable Incident Rate (ORIR), Pick/Ship Accuracy, and Carton per Man Hour (CPMH) metrics. The goal was to shift the focus from cost to productivity. The team held daily face-to-face meetings to review and discuss Root Cause Counter Measure (RCCM) opportunities. Just by tracking KPIs, the team improved safety, productivity and fulfilment quality.

3. Revamped the safety incident reporting program.

To reduce the number of safety incidents, we turned control of the incident reporting system over to the team members. While many think that the safety manager "owns" safety, the desired state is for everyone to own safety. To facilitate the shift, we set up systems to engage employees and created a safety council responsible for developing policies, reviewing incidents, and owning floor messaging.

4. Updated the Warehouse Management System (WMS) and codes.

To improve output quality, we set up a new Warehouse Management System and changed all codes in the system, effectively automating the entire distribution system. Previously, warehouse staff would use a paper list to pick products for orders and put them in boxes to ship to customers.

Now, the new WMS generates labels and scans products, associating each product with the correct shipper. The new compliance scanning and case picking system ensures quality at the source, establishing standards for field picking. It also enables supervisors to staff operations more efficiently. For the first time, the team can ensure that only what is supposed to ship goes out. No more, no less.

5. Equipped supervisors to train hourly associates on Lean practices.

This step aimed to engage both leadership and operations teams by holding formal classroom training sessions every week and quizzes/exercises to ensure comprehension.

6. Implemented eight safety and ergonomics improvements warehouse management.

To further improve safety, the team targeted the department with the highest personal risk; pallet building. The team identified risks and reconfigured the space to engineer out risk and build in ergonomics. This entailed changing the heights of where products and pallets were located and moving tools closer to workers to minimize reaching, bending at the waist, heavy lifting and other hazards.

7. Eliminated unnecessary quality checks.

Eliminating waste is a key Lean principle. Waste takes many forms, including unnecessary processes. In that spirit, the team replaced an ineffective quality check; weighing pallets with compliance scanning. Instead of measuring quality by weight, the team scanned boxes, cartons and pallets to make sure the right number of parts was packed inside.

8. Reallocated associates from QA to more added job.

Now that the automated compliance scanning system eliminating the need to weigh pallets to check for quality, the team was able to re-allocated resources to build quality in rather than inspect for it. The workers who had been weighing cartons and pallets, both ergonomically risky activities, were moved to other functions; doubling down on root cause countermeasures as part of a warehouse action (SWAT) team, focused on identifying waste and inefficiency and eliminating it. In a Non-Lean environment, the workers would have been let go. In a Lean environment, they received 30 hours of training, and returned to the floor with new skills, in a new capacity.

9. Created lane assignments for Pallet Build associates

Previously, there wasn't a structured system for assigning pallets to lanes for picking and pallet building. Parts moved randomly to operators by conveyor belt, forcing workers to run around and crisscross lanes to fulfil orders. To streamline operations, the team assigned workers to dedicated lanes. This not only eliminated unnecessary movement, it improved safety and throughput.

10. Established performance reviews for salaried leads and managers

To create a performance-based culture, the team established one-on-one talent reviews for salaried leads and managers. In the reviews, leaders were asked to identify their goals, skills, and responsibilities, and help build a talent development plan, tying personal incentives to team performance. The new system not only eliminated favouritism and empowered employees, it improved accountability.

By fast-tracking improvements in all ten of these areas, the company completed a transformation in less than a year that normally would take much longer.

Chapter 21: From Lean to Lasting

For companies seeking large-scale operational improvements, all roads lead to Toyota. Each year, thousands of executives tour its facilities to learn how lean production; the operational and organizational innovations the automaker pioneered might help their own companies. During the past 20 years, lean has come, along with Six Sigma, one of two kinds of prominent performance-improvement programs adopted by global manufacturing and, more recently, service companies. Recently, organizations as diverse as steelmakers, insurance companies, and public-sector agencies have benefited from "leaning" their operations with Toyota's now-classic approach; eliminating waste, variability, and inflexibility.

Yet in our experience, organizations overlook up to half of the potential savings when they implement or expand operational-improvement programs inspired by lean, Six Sigma, or both. Some companies set their sights too low; others falter by implementing lean and other performance-enhancing tools without recognizing how existing performance-management systems or employee mind-sets might undermine them. Still others underestimate the level of senior-management involvement required; for example, they delegate responsibility for change programs to their lean experts or Six Sigma black belts practitioners who are technically skilled but often lack the authority, capabilities, or numbers to make change stick.

The broader challenge underlying such problems is integrating the better-known "hard" operational tools and approaches such as just-in-time production with the "soft" side, including the development of leaders who can help teams to continuously identify and make efficiency improvements, link and align the boardroom with the shop floor, and build the technical and interpersonal skills that make efficiency benefits real. Mastering lean's softer side is difficult because it forces all employees to commit themselves to new ways of thinking and working. Toyota remains the exemplar; while many companies can replicate its lean technology, success on the softer side often eludes them.

Some companies, however, overcome the challenges and get more from their operational-improvement programs. Against a backdrop of growing economic uncertainty, their success can be a source of inspiration and enlightenment for industrial and service companies and for public and social-sector organizations looking to extract greater value from these efforts.

Soft is hard

Making operational change stick is difficult. Operations typically account for the largest number of a company's employees and the widest variation in skill levels. Units often are scattered across dozens or even hundreds of sites throughout the world, function independently, and have distinct corporate cultures particularly if Merger and Acquisition has fuelled a company's growth. Each facility may specialize in different products or services and face unique pressures from customers, competitors, and regulators. These factors complicate efforts to design, execute, and scale operational-improvement programs.

A better approach to scaling

Consequently, many companies emphasize the technical aspects of their programs over the organizational ones. That approach is understandable. Technical solutions are objective and straightforward; analytical solutions to operational problems abound in lean and Six Sigma tool kits; and companies make significant investments to train experts who know how to apply them. What is more, the tools and experts actually are invaluable in diagnosing and improving operational performance.

Overlooking the softer side, however, drastically lowers any initiative's odds of success. Some companies, for example, rush to implement the tool kit without ensuring that their employees including managers are prepared to work and lead in new and different ways. In such cases, "initiative fatigue" and even distrust may set in, and efficiency gains fizzle out as the black belts move on to other projects.

At times, such an improvement initiative first appears to be successful but is later found to be insufficient to meet the company's main objectives. An aerospace manufacturer, for example, wanted to increase production of a product with rapidly growing sales. The company's lean experts, assigned to plan and run the initiative, quickly identified productivity enhancement opportunities and began conducting kaizen projects. On the surface, the program was working; but management's inattention to the softer side created difficulties.

Since the program's goals were not adequately defined or communicated by senior managers, the experts focused on what they could achieve primarily easy wins, including technical changes to redesign assembly processes and to improve the effectiveness of certain machines. In retrospect, these changes, while broadly useful, did little to help meet growing demand for the product. Meanwhile, some of the company's salespeople, long frustrated with what they saw as the shortcomings of the operations group, began circumventing the production scheduling system in order to speed their own products through the queue. That undercut many of the efficiency gains the experts managed to create.

The result, in fact, was chaos; line workers later showed executives a schedule indicating that one machine, chosen at random, was to perform 250 hours of work during an 8-hour shift. This revelation spurred the executives to refocus the program, investigate the organizational factors behind the difficulties, and ultimately identify much more far-reaching solutions; starting with an effort to get sales and operations to collaborate in setting production priorities and to work together on a daily basis.

Getting started: Set high aspirations

Such examples show that neglecting the organizational components of an operational transformation can delay or even derail it. Top companies, by contrast, attend to the softer elements of an initiative throughout its whole course, starting with the earliest, aspiration-setting phases, when senior leaders identify the key goals and start to communicate them. That helps companies to establish a stronger foundation for change and to set more achievable, and often much higher, ambitions than they otherwise could. A better understanding of the cultural starting point enables top companies to determine where they should focus at the beginning of a program, when to implement its various elements, and how to achieve their goals.

Consider the experience of a North American power generator that used cultural insights to combat scepticism about the scope of the efficiency improvements attainable in a nascent initiative. This kind of doubt is common when companies lack a self-evident catalyst for change say, a takeover or a looming bankruptcy. The power generator responded by sending its managers to visit a company, in another process-intensive industry, that had recently implemented a lean program. There the managers saw similar improvements in action and heard the enthusiasm that line managers and union leaders expressed for them. That experience was instrumental in helping the managers address their own employees' uncertainties about how much improvement was possible.

Likewise, greater attention to corporate culture helped a global chemical company launch an efficiency-improvement program across its network of 300 plants. The company's abiding respect for science and for highly educated experts at first biased managers in favour of solutions based on new technology rather than line-level process improvements. After conducting a pilot project, however, executives saw that about 60 percent of the value it generated came from new work processes, not new and more efficient machines. That realization changed the design of the program and raised its goals in some cases, by a factor of three. The company now expects the program to have an annual impact of more than $1 billion.

By contrast, companies that misread employee mind-sets and other cultural elements squander time and resources. A large logistics group that tried to overhaul its transport network, for example, overlooked the way years of inadequate capital investment would affect the program's ramp-up. Why did the company make this mistake? It turned out that the gradual decline in capital spending had, over time, led the company's maintenance workers to assume that their skills weren't valued, so the seriousness of many problems had gone unreported. The company's executives found that the goals of the program were therefore initially unattainable.

Making change happen

After accounting for the way culture and other organizational factors will affect the goals of a program, leading companies put what they learn into action. They reap bigger, more sustainable benefits by balancing the program's hard and soft elements and developing their line managers' lean leadership skills.

Take a balanced approach

The experience of a North American distribution company that sought to address higher customer expectations and eroding margins in its network of 70 distribution centres shows the virtues of a more balanced approach. The company looked beyond technical changes, to the ways that organizational structures and processes and even the mind-sets of employees could affect its ability to meet the goals it set.

Managers have feelings too

Operations leaders identified labour balancing as an important technical improvement; they planned to create teams that would combine two roles "pickers," who located products to fill customer orders, and "packers," who loaded orders onto trucks. The new system was supposed to increase productivity by redistributing labour more efficiently to meet shifting demand. The company didn't stop at such technical fixes, however; in parallel, it revamped its performance management system to encourage the new ways of working. Pickers had been measured quantitatively (primarily on speed, not accuracy), packers qualitatively or not at all, depending on the site. Executives now combined the existing metrics into a team-based system aimed at helping the company's trucks depart on time. This change not only balanced speed and accuracy but also pushed workers to collaborate and to focus on a common goal. In addition, the company created a prominent visual tracking system to reinforce the new behaviour by showing employees, in real time, when shifting workloads required their immediate attention.

Changing the mind-sets of workers proved critical as well. Many workers in both groups, which had viewed each other as rivals, were company veterans who strongly identified with their roles. Pickers had traditionally felt superior, since they typically worked alone and could be quite successful with individualized approaches, whereas packing was more standardized. Recognizing that such factors would breed resentment if ignored, the company provided supervisors with on-the-job training in interpersonal skills; including coaching and the art of having difficult conversations in the weeks before making the technical changes. The supervisors later reported that the integration and timing of these elements helped the program succeed by instilling in them the influencing skills needed to highlight the new system's benefits (both to their teams and to individual workers) and to convince doubters that the changes were important. (Often, companies undermine their performance-improvement programs by introducing otherwise useful training elements at inappropriate times for instance, several months before the implementation of the program, when its goals may not be clear to the trainees.)

Within six months, the distribution centres that had adopted the new system were 10 to 15 percent more productive, on-time deliveries were up 5 to 10 percent, and errors reported by customers were down by as much as one-third. Moreover, a survey of workers found that their satisfaction levels had risen by 10 percent. Subsequent analysis suggested that about half of the productivity gains were attributable to the softer elements and about half to technical changes, such as more efficient warehouse layouts.

Lead through the line

At the heart of most big operational-improvement efforts are a company's black belts, lean sensei, and other change agents brought in to lead programs, spur new ideas and practices, and champion the mind-set of continuous improvement. Companies typically follow this template because it appears easier than significantly involving their line leadership. Shop floor deadlines are fierce, line leaders are busy, and many of them lack the skills to direct large initiatives. Some executives therefore argue that line managers should focus instead on day-to-day concerns.

Yet that is a mistake. Large-scale change requires all employees from the C-suite to the shop floor to think and work differently. Companies that use only experts to orchestrate change programs may be fairly successful. Still, by outsourcing the responsibility for initiatives (and, by extension, the underlying ideas) to experts, even their own, these companies often miss significant opportunities. Moreover, once the low-hanging fruit is gone, such efforts often lose steam as employees slip into old habits; experts may convey the new language or technical tools but rarely the desire to change behaviour permanently, nor can these experts build the organizational capabilities that permanent change requires.

Lean leaders can cultivate six habits to model desired mind-sets and behaviour for their employees.

By contrast, when a company shifts the attention of its line managers away from fire-fighting, develops their leadership capabilities, and expects more from them, the gains are bigger and longer lasting. Experts still play a vital catalyzing role, of course, but now as teachers, coaches, and counsellors. Line managers are better placed to lead change efforts and to serve as long-term role models and should be held accountable for doing so.

The North American power generator mentioned previously learned this lesson several months into its improvement initiative as executives sought to fire up the program's momentum. This company had sent its operations experts into field offices, so they could work closely with employees at individual plants, where they had enjoyed significant success. Senior executives, however, observed that enthusiasm and engagement soon started fading among the line workers. In the words of one executive, "They were still coming to work from the neck down."

Senior executives therefore vowed to move the effort "out of the office and into the line." The company created a "lean leader" profile a list of desirable characteristics, such as problem-solving, coaching, and analytical skills. Management then created a curriculum to build them through the "forum and field" approach; hands-on training and coaching forums (on topics such as performance management, time management, and problem solving) followed by practice in real-world applications.

To ensure that everyone understood the permanence of the changes, the company made weekly one-on-one training and coaching sessions a part of its line managers' jobs. Shift schedules were adjusted to incorporate coaching into the workers' routines. (While most executives recognize the value of coaching, many fail to institutionalize it, thus unintentionally making it seem less important.) These brief sessions allowed workers to celebrate successes, share ideas, and measure progress in achieving the program's goals. Soon, employees began carrying index cards listing the improvement priorities they had spotted during the previous week.

The cards and related conversations generated creative ideas including a new way to keep coal dry when it was shipped to the company's power plants. These and other line-led improvements helped significantly to raise the plant's output and, subsequently, to cut its fuel costs. More important, the training efforts enhanced the skills of managers, enabling them to become the foundation for a host of additional improvements.

To get the most from large operational-improvement programs, top companies look beyond the technical aspects of lean and Six Sigma and embrace the softer side. Complementing the development of technical skills with a focus on the organizational capabilities that make efficiency benefits real can help companies to achieve more substantial, sustainable, and scalable results.

Chapter 22: Conclusion

The retail industry consistently introduces certain fleeting industry buzzwords. Like fashion trends, these buzzwords are often short-lived, and sometimes give cringe-worthy memories upon reflection; but the ones that have potential longevity... they become timeless. Like a classic Chanel bag, they leave lasting impressions, and become industry fixtures that businesses model their plan around.

In the retail industry notably, often times, the economic zeitgeist determines the landscape of business trends. During the technology bubble in the 1990's, the economy enjoyed an influx of wealth, and brands expanded both their brick and mortar storefronts, as well as introducing their online platform.

In comparison, Lean Retail is a term manifested through the recession. It turns the traditional business model on its head. Taught in business schools everywhere, the curriculum stated that you needed a comprehensive business plan that allowed for little to no wiggle room. It was simple; acquire capital, locate a brick and mortar space, and open up shop. Brands focused on the offline environment first, and the online later.

After the economy took a downturn in the middle of 2000's, brands had to strategise and adapt quickly. Storefronts closed, and online-only brand presence surged. Emerging brands were discouraged to open brick and mortar spaces, and turn their attention towards the potential global consumer they can reach on the internet.

Lean Retail incorporates tactics used for savvy technology start-ups in Silicon Valley to transform the way retail utilizes their current business strategy. It focuses on smarter growth with low cost experimentation and more intuitive instead of stringent planning. Lean Retail is an adaptable model that emphasizes melding the online retail model, and taking it to an offline test market.

The four suggested principles below are crucial to the survival of a retailer.

1. Learn faster: Opening up a brick and mortar outlet is often costly, and highly risky. There is a large chance that the location was not the best place to reach your target demographic resulting in low foot traffic. This leads to a sharp decline in net profit, and coupled with the skyrocketing commercial rental prices, businesses can quickly succumb to shuttering their windows. Lean Retail allows you to "test" a location by researching temporary vacant spaces for your intended consumer base. This arms you with the knowledge that the storefront will provide you with guaranteed foot traffic. By testing and researching a neighbourhood first, the brand receives better customer feedback to possibly apply the business in a more permanent brick and mortar location. Lean Retail becomes less risky, a huge positive with emerging brands working on a limited financial budget.

2. Versatility: Lean Retail can be applied towards a plethora of companies, and industries. A viable option for an artist who wishes to open up their own independent gallery without the costly overhead, or a technology brand that is launching a new product and wants to introduce it in a physical environment. Restaurants, home furnishings, accessories and small niche brands, and even online collaborative maker markets like Etsy can benefit from opening up a Lean Retail concept. The unifying factor in these variety of businesses is that temporary spaces are versatile, and since they are turn-key, can be transformed to your brands needs without renovating the entire space.

3. Lower risk: Lean Retail allows for a brand to test out a market in a high-volume location without confining themselves to a long term lease. They are then able to insert themselves in locations that they may not have otherwise considered. For example, Storefront also includes client comments that have previously utilized a potential space. You are able to see what worked (and what may not have) to make more educated, and less costly choices for your Lean Retail venture.

4. Shorter-term: Most people take a sharp intake of air when signing their lives away for a long term lease. The beauty of Lean Retail is that the lease terms are negotiable. From one day, to one year, there is an option that will perfectly suit your intended needs and forecast for your company to test out a space/target market. This also allows for placing yourself in high peak seasons that will generate the most revenue for your brand. The holiday season is a huge opportunity to apply Lean Retail for your business, but get creative. Your brand may be best suited adjacent to a large musical festival. Or perhaps injected near a sports stadium for a major event/game.

Lean Retail isn't an industry buzzword. It is an intelligent business tactic that gives your company the flexibility it needs in this evolving economic climate. Much like the coveted and classic Chanel bag, Lean Retail is never regretted by those who buy into this model.

Know, Understand and Involve Your Customers. It's a given that without customers you will have no business. You need to know what they want and how they want it not just now, but in the future to stay ahead of the game. Ask them questions such as; would they recommend your business to others without hesitation. If not, ask them what they think you need to do better.

Good Luck!!

www.ingramcontent.com/pod-product-compliance
Lightning Source LLC
Chambersburg PA
CBHW051716170526
45167CB00002B/687